VOLTAIRE'S GARDEN

A MEMOIR OF COBARGO

ISOBEL BLACKTHORN

For Cobargo, a working village nestled in the rolling foothills of the Great Dividing Range in Australia's southeast.

PROLOGUE
A GARDEN IN GHANA

I force open my eyes and throw off the covers. Daylight filters through shuttered windows. Before I rise, I take in the bright-blue walls of this sparsely furnished room, walls that at night crawl with large spiders. I'm amazed none had bothered to crawl over me.

I wrap myself in a sarong and join Colin in the living room. We breakfast, shower, and pack in silence, not wanting to leave as we close the door behind us.

Despite the early hour, sunlight belts down on my hat through a dusty, smoke haze. It's February 2001 and the Harmattan, a seasonal wind blowing Saharan dust into the tropical rain forests of West Africa's coastal fringe, has come early again and is set to last weeks longer than it used to. Fires smoulder on the forest fringes, the forest that is receding year on year, leaving parched earth behind. The World Bank funded saw mill somewhere up the road isn't helping. Neither is climate change.

Eight-thirty, and I feel like another bucket shower. Heading towards the school we walk along the main street of Pampawie, a remote village situated far up the tongue of land between the River Volta and the Togoan border in Ghana's mid-northeast. Pampawie, a ribbon of mud-brick dwellings with no telecommunications and an unreliable electricity supply. Here and there a shade tree rises out of the parched earth, its foliage offering momentary relief from the sun. Deep dish drains flank the street. When the rains come, they come heavy. There are no cars. Just chickens scratching, dogs lying in the shade.

Women in brightly-coloured dresses and headscarves are gathered near the communal kitchens in the market square. They watch us as we walk by. Four girls balancing large bowls of water on their heads approach and we move out of their way. Old men sitting under corrugated-iron verandas take sidelong glances at us before carrying on chatting or dreaming.

Agnes and Genevieve join us and walk to either side of me, their straight backs and swinging hips evidence of their female power and self-esteem. Walking between them with their arms brushing mine and I'm awash with filial affection as I struggle to match their gait, but I am out of shape and suffering badly from influenza. My guts are not faring well either. Was it the lettuce leaf I ate back in Accra, or the Ghanaian beer? Either way I, along with my colleague and fellow teacher Colin, have been punishing the pit toilet provided for our personal use by our host, John.

Agnes touches my arm as we near the centre of the village, pointing to her home. She smiles a sweet, closed-mouth smile. I nod and smile in silence. We have become good friends, Genevieve, Agnes and I. Like soul-sisters with a bent for laughter, in one week we have bypassed cultural and language differences through a shared, and perhaps a little wicked, sense of humour. Colin has become the butt of a whole string of jokes, his English demeanour and lack of physical flexibility compared to his African counterparts arousing great merriment and an intimate common ground between us. Luckily, good-natured Colin joins in the merriment. Looking back, I am sure it was those moments of mirth and intimacy that made my legs walk the distance to the school each day without collapsing.

As we approach the school buildings my pace quickens, drawn by the shade of the deep veranda facing the quadrangle, and my special seat, a comfy armchair covered in protective if sweat-inducing plastic. Students congregate outside, lining up in their orange and brown uniforms for the assembly. A woman approaches with a platter of orange slices. I slurp and dribble for a while, the fresh-picked taste compulsive. Agnes looks on and then touches my arm again.

'Isobel, too many oranges are not good for the stomach.'

'Next time I will come in mango season,' I reply with a grin, little knowing there would be no next time.

Colin sits beside me and fiddles with the digital video camera.

We had arrived in Ghana two weeks earlier, ambassadors from our own high school, Polesworth, a village near Birmingham. We came here to formalise the school link I founded through the auspices of the On The Line millennium project established by Oxfam and other charities to link schools and communities on the Greenwich meridian. To kick off the link we agreed to create a garden in each school and I secured funding from the British Council for a teacher exchange on that basis.

With the last of the students assembled, the principal Peter starts another round of speeches. After a week of meetings, discussions and celebrations, each event prefaced by speeches, I am relieved this will be the last. Public speaking is not my forte, especially unscripted, and the wretched way I have felt this week has rendered me almost mute. Thank heavens for Colin, whose easy style and charm, in combination with the loud voice of an industrial arts teacher, fulfilled our public speaking obligations magnificently. I just smiled and nodded.

This time we are not required to say anything. With the talking over, the children sing. With one voice, so rich, sweet and melodic, they bid us farewell. I am mesmerized and my jaw drops a little in wonder at the harmonious sound I hear from the mouths of these sweet children. My eyes well with tears as I stare into their faces beaded with perspiration, their eyes filled with hope. Will the garden help them to grow as people? Will they come to understand the deep power that comes from planting a seed, nurturing a seedling, watching it flourish and flower, and harvesting its fruit? Will they make the connection between a seed and themselves? It is a big ask. A metaphor only exists when we recognize it so. Without this recognition, this insightful layering of meaning remains hidden from our minds, its fluttering wings tiny ripples of knowing in our hearts alone.

The students head back to their classrooms. There is no sign of the car that is due to collect us for the drive back to Accra so Peter suggests a quick last look at the main purpose of our visit – the site for the garden that will commemorate our link. I leave the shade reluctantly and follow Colin and Peter as they stroll across the quadrangle to the chosen site. Back at Polesworth we have earmarked a site for a garden too. The gardens will symbolise the link, providing in plants a constant reminder of the new collaboration between our two wildly disparate high schools – Polesworth, which boasts a state-of-the-art drama theatre and new computer lab, and Pampawie, which is sadly short of chalk, and where the children learn to count with stones and write with sticks.

Peter explains the need for a fence to keep the animals out as I look once more at the perimeter of stones surrounding a large flat rectangle of dry grass, a long way from my early morning vision. However the garden turns out to be, it is already a source of great inspiration, capturing the imagination and enthusiasm of the teaching staff at Pampawie. Gardens are special places, each one the result of human creation. As a symbol of a link between two schools I can think of no better way to begin the linking process.

Our car pulls into the school grounds. The driver smiles and shakes our hands. It is time to leave. I glance at Colin. He fumbles with the camera so I turn to take one last look around. My eyes settle on the school's only garbage bin, a small hand-woven basket nestling in the crotch of a trifurcated log planted in the ground.

My heart is heavy. I want to go home and not go home all at once. I want the comfort of my own bed, but I want to take the generosity of spirit I found here with me, the spirit of Africa that has captured me the way it has countless others. In song, in tears, in laughter and in tragedy, this spirit lives. I cannot bear the thought of all the human suffering that goes on in countries like Ghana with a history blighted by slavery and colonization, countries rendered crushingly poor through the economic processes of unfairness, where the economic dictates of a few wealthy individuals and corporations in the North can render so many in the South so economically insecure. Would that I could wave a magic wand and fix it all right now, but I can't. Would that I could bottle the spirit of Africa and take it home as an elixir but I cannot do that either.

All I can do is hope the link would lessen some of the unfairness.

Issues of fairness, or social justice, are never far from my mind. I visit them on a daily basis in my classroom. Like the Ancient Greek philosopher Epicurus, or Buddha, I believe a moderate life based around considered personal limits is the best kind of life to lead. To reasonably know when we've had enough and before we indulge in excess is a happy life, a pleasurable life, one not driven by desires for wealth and power. I hope my Ghanaian friends will carry into their hearts and minds the simple pleasures found in their garden, of watching a plant grow, of smelling a flower, tasting a fruit, listening to birds, watching insects and soaking in the atmosphere. I hope that both gardens will help to transform lives.

CHAPTER ONE

CREATING A NEW DREAM

'You must have a magnificent estate,' said Candide to the Turk.

'Only twenty acres,' replied the Turk. 'My children help me to farm it, and we find that the work banishes those three great evils, boredom, vice and poverty.'

CANDIDE

Blackbutt Drive was a cul-de-sac. At the end, a granite boulder held open a farm gate. Filled with excitement and fear I walked through the gate as if crossing a threshold, about build a new home and garden on fifteen acres of fallow cattle paddock. I had a want-list seared into my mind and the determination of Hercules to make it happen. There would be vegetable gardens, herb gardens and orchards of fruit and nut trees all grown organically; chickens, sheep and trees for firewood; and native shrubberies and flowers everywhere. We'd have solar panels and a windmill. And guest accommodation, bed-and-breakfast style. A model of self-sufficiency, a source of inspiration for others. I was *agent provocateur* again. Only this time, in Cobargo, a quaint Australian village on the south coast of New South Wales. A logical if unlikely choice of retreat. Logical, in that I was following a family tradition set in the 1970s when my maternal grandmother built a house there. My mother and sister did the same in the 1980s. Unlikely, in that as my family called Cobargo home, I had wandered the world looking for mine.

I'd had little expectation of staying this time. Then I met Greg, a Slovenian Australian with a degree in philosophy. Originally from Sydney, Greg moved down the coast a decade earlier searching for a better life. After three failed ventures he bought a dilapidated cottage in the village, did odd-jobs for cash and received a modest stipend for editing a local magazine. The day we met, I was drawn to him immediately. With him, I saw a chance of permanence. After fifty-five addresses, I wanted an immovable physical centre, somewhere for my daughters to grow into adults, a solid foundation for a new life. So I married him.

I strolled down the driveway to the house site. The autumn sun shone through a stand of red gums in the far corner of the block. Luminescing wispy mists hovered over the dams, creeks and gullies to the west. Above the mists, where the mountains rose to meet the escarpment of the Great Dividing Range, the forests glowed mellow orange. A view captivating at any time, now splendidly silhouetted against the lightening sky, revealing in relief the curvaceous layering of peaks, ridges, spurs and saddles, and gorges and ravines. It was exhilarating, a confirmation of a decision well-made.

Greg was already at work. He'd driven up at dawn. He was on his knees scoring a square into hard clay on the house pad, his muscle-bound torso bundled in a sheepskin jacket, his elfin face buried in a balaclava. Having spent our savings on the excavations we couldn't afford to hire a back hoe. We were doing things manually while we waited for the sale of Greg's cottage to complete. Greg would most likely have dug the footings regardless. It was his way. He had a Luddite approach to modern life. 'Why use a mechanical device when peasants have for centuries coped well enough with simple hand tools?' he would say. For him, empowerment was gripping his hoe.

He continued to make hard jabs with the corner of a spade.

Behind him, obscuring the view of the village was a heap of sun-baked soil and another of sand, rubble and broken concrete – the remains of someone's former driveway. Greg wanted the concrete for crazy paving.

To the west, a felled apple gum lay in its tangle of branches and leaves, a sacrifice to make way for the septic system. To the northwest, the view was unmolested by the chaos of the build. Two mounds of clay and scores of topsoil humps littered the north-facing hillside that fell away gently towards a gully at the bottom. Our land rose up a short distance beyond the gully before meeting the neighbour's fence. On the eastern rise, excavations for the house, rainwater tank and garage had gouged gnarly clay batters into the hillside. Situated below the house stood a twenty-thousand-gallon tank shining industrial silver and ready to receive rainwater. And directly behind Greg was the temporary home he'd spent all summer erecting – candy pink bathroom, yellow-ochre caravans and a double garage. The whole building site looked ghastly, made worse by the colour choices I had applied to the bathroom and caravans. I had to conjure an image of the site's future magnificence just to look at it.

I joined Greg on the house pad. 'You've arrived.'

'I had things to do.'

'The footings have to be four-hundred-millimetre square,' he said in his typically dour way. He'd felt daunted by the build from day one.

'Okay.'

'Dug to a depth of two-hundred millimetres.'

'Doesn't sound too bad.'

'And there are one-hundred-and-five of them.'

He thrust his spade into the line he'd scored. It went in about an inch.

'It was never going to be easy,' I said. 'Where should I start?'

'Anywhere you like.'

He'd begun in the hardest corner, where the excavator had exposed a sub-soil of decomposing granite. I started work on a footing nearby. I scored a perimeter line then rammed my spade into the ground. It made a barely visible dent. I chipped, levered and scraped the beginnings of a hole. I'd made a slightly more visible dent.

'I think I need help,' I said.

Greg peered over at me through his balaclava and grabbed his crow bar.

'Stand back.'

He pounded the ground, sending a flurry of dust and tiny fragments into my face. I blinked and shook my head.

'Stand further back,' he said.

I obeyed and he continued pounding.

'That should do you,' he said and walked back to his hole.

I trowelled out the debris. The hole was now ten centimetres deep.

'At least they can't get any harder,' I said, trying to sound encouraging.

'They won't get much easier either.'

The day warmed. Back on my feet with the spade, then on

my knees with my trowel. Spade, crow bar, trowel; spade, crow bar, trowel. Four holes partially dug and it was lunchtime. We perched on the slabs of broken concrete and ate cheese sandwiches, staring blankly at the site.

By dusk we'd managed ten holes.

Two weeks and five cubic metres of concrete later, we stared at one hundred and five concrete pads, those on the perimeter with steel straps sprouting from their centres. I was hardly to know it then, that I would be staring at those concrete pads for another six months.

I'd moved into Greg's old and rundown cottage three years earlier with my eleven-year-old daughters, Sarah and Mary, and our tortoiseshell cat, Pickles. Greg had already transformed his half-acre garden from a rough patch of overgrown lawn into a series of terraces edged with massive granite boulders and broken concrete. But the cottage was sinking into the ground on its hundred-year-old, rotting red-gum stumps. Storm water silting from the dirt road above had buried sections of sub-floor. The roof leaked, windows hung crookedly, and the closed-in verandas were in serious disrepair.

It wasn't long before we re-stumped. We shovelled out from under the house barrows and barrows full of soil. We used the soil to top-dress the lawn, increasing the level of the whole block about ten centimetres. Greg raised the bearers on car jacks and removed the stumps one by one. I dug the footings to a depth of a metre or more using a handle-less shovel and a trowel. I enjoyed the work. It was a much-needed break from the doctoral thesis I'd started shortly after my return to Cobargo.

I was researching the interplay between literal and metaphoric interpretations of esoteric texts, focusing on the teachings of Theosophist Alice A. Bailey. I had three years to prove my point. Three years paid by the government. Handsomely too. By the same government that refused to recognize my teaching qualification from the UK which meant I could not teach in state schools in Australia unless I retrained. After leaving the highwater mark of the Ghana Link, I wasn't about to do that.

When I returned to my studies Greg demolished walls and re-laid floors all around me. He poured enormous creative energy into the renovations. He put his heart into every stick of timber, his thought in every fine detail, from the original red gum wall studs to the original stringy-bark floorboards. We bought more floorboards recycled from an abandoned shearing shed in the Snowy Mountains, framing timber from another old high-country building, and one massively long four by two from Cobargo's old Butter Factory.

My thesis progressed in parallel with the renovations. I puzzled ideas while Greg puzzled room designs. When I re-structured chapters Greg was moving interior walls. And when my supervisor told me to add a meta-theory, something to hang all my ideas from and hold the whole lot together, Greg re-roofed. Whatever I did in my thesis, Greg was doing something similar with the building. It felt magical. But as both projects neared completion I began to worry about the future. My doctorate looked set to lead nowhere, the topic too obscure, my approach uncomfortably radical and academic postings in the field few. We'd been living off my scholarship so that Greg could focus on the renovations. But that would run out next February. Nine short months away. What next? – Unemployment benefits? Greg wasn't bothered. He had a take-it-as-it-comes approach to life. But I *was* bothered. I needed another project, something to justify leaving behind the Ghana link, something to justify staying in Cobargo.

I came up with the idea, not exactly a tree-change, more a tree side-step, during a mid-winter walk around Cobargo's former golf course.

The evening was still. Leaving the cottage unlocked, we walked through the wisteria-laden lichgate and joined a track near the sports ground's toilet block. The track, a mown strip, coursed up the hill to the north, zigzagging round the disused fairways and greens. I wanted a brisk walk but Greg felt like a stroll. He liked to observe the minutiae of life.

Five minutes into our walk I heard, 'Isobel. Look. Isn't it pretty.'

I halted my stride and turned back. He was on his haunches looking into the pasture.

'Come closer. It's exquisite.'

I bent down beside him. He pointed at a tiny star-like flower nestling among native grasses, six milky-white petals splayed open to reveal a bright-yellow centre.

'See the purple halo radiating little lines up the spine of each petal?' he said.

I peered closer. It was so delicate, not showy like many cultivated flowers, and it was so small someone like me would tread on it on their way past.

I hadn't managed more than ten paces before Greg stopped me again. This time he'd spotted a wedge-tail eagle circling in the sky high above us. Before long a pair of mud-larks chased away the eagle with an angry flurry of wing-flapping and high-pitched cries.

'That's pee wee for eagle,' Greg said.

We headed towards the cemetery, crossing the rickety wooden bridge littered with overgrown brambles growing in the creek below and following the rise to the crest. This was my favourite part of the walk. The path turns sharply west, affording an admirable view of Cobargo snuggling in the hills that undulate to the western ranges. A view to quiet the heart.

I threw my arms out wide. 'I could never leave this place. It's so gorgeous.'

'And Cobargo's the perfect size,' Greg said. 'That's what makes this view so charming – Cobargo'.

I glanced across the highway. Fenced in the shape of a pointed boot was the land my mother used to entice me to leave England. Then the land belonged to her. Now I owned half of it. She was keen to sell me the other half.

I turned to catch Greg's eye. 'I'd love to buy out my mother's share of the land.'

'Do it.'

'And build.'

He hesitated. 'To do that we'd have to sell the cottage.'

'I know. But just imagine how self-sufficient we could be with all that land.'

'Build a whole house?' He frowned. 'I'm not sure I'd want to take that on. Renovating is enough building for me.'

'But everyone says that building is easier and quicker than renovating. Just think – new materials. No de-nailing. No sanding off old paint.'

'I don't think I can do it. It's a question of scale.'

'Of course you can. Look what you've done with the renovations.'

'Isobel, you've used the wrong tense. I'm still renovating.'

'Not for much longer.'

Greg sighed. He turned his back to me and gazed at the sunset. I persisted.

'And I'll have finished my thesis. I can be of more help.'

He stood beside a small-framed light-weight woman who couldn't fork the ground without hurting her back and was prone to muscle spasms that left her prostrate on the sofa for days. But I was determined. I looked past Cobargo at the mountains. Dumpling Ridge was bathed in a soft back-light, silhouetted against the blue-grey of the ranges behind. Stunning, but a view wasn't enough to base a major life decision on. I had to find other ways to persuade Greg.

'Look, we don't want to live in a city, but there's no work for us around here. We have to do *something*.'

'That something, as you put it, will turn up.'

'Will it? We could make the land work for us instead. Think of all the fruit and vegetables we could grow. And we'd have chickens, maybe goats or sheep. And olives, avocados and almonds. All that food!'

'Won't pay the bills, Isobel.'

'We could try out cash crops for that.'

Greg paused. 'We *could* provide guest accommodation.'

'Run a bed and breakfast?'

He'd mentioned this before. Becoming a guesthouse proprietor held no appeal. All that cleaning, bed-changing, washing and cooking. I'd feel like a lackey. But we did live in a tourist area. And it was a way of introducing strangers to a different lifestyle. If that's what it would take to convince Greg, then I'd do it.

'Okay.'

'Okay?' Greg turned to face me. 'Are you sure?'

'That way we might have enough to fulfil our needs.'

Enough for us would not be very much at all. Others might see themselves as battlers in spite of owning a four-wheel drive and a swimming pool. We were different. We had humble aspirations and simple needs. We loved buying things second-hand. We made things, fixed things and did without things. Our leisure time was spent in the garden. We were the antithesis of consumerism; we were preservers. I preserved food and Greg preserved everything he could lay his hands on

– timber, fence posts, furniture, old tools, bits of wire, and anything in the garden. Give Greg a junk pile and he'd turn it, in time, to myriad uses.

Heading for home, the idea quickly became a vision. We imagined our cottage garden and multiplied it by ten. Individual trees became orchards, an average-sized vegetable garden, a series of sweeping terraces. As our walk neared its end we dreamt up a castle with all of its grounds complete, and then we decided to give it a name.

Thinking of the phones, faxes and modems struck by lightning around here I came up with Lightning Ridge.

'Who on earth would book into a guest house with a name like that.'

'Dun' roamin',' I said, thinking of my own nomadic life. 'Greg's Nest?'

We both laughed at that.

'It has to be a name that reflects what we are trying to achieve,' Greg said.

'One that speaks of the garden and the views then.'

'And one that captures our beliefs.'

'You remember how we were going to erect little plaques in our garden, like Schopenhauer's Shed and Descartes' Dog House? We should think of something along those lines.'

'Nietzsche's Nook, err, Hegel's Heaven.'

'Hume's Hovel.'

'Don't be ridiculous.'

'What about Voltaire's Garden?'

'Did he have a garden?'

'Voltaire? No idea.'

I discovered soon after that Voltaire did have a garden. Later in his life when he went into exile, first at Les Délices, a property he rented near Geneva, and then at Ferney, just below the French Alps. He was a lover of fresh produce. He grew herbs. Voltaire's garden had lavender, rue and hyssop, basil, sage and salad burnet, and rosemary, tarragon and thyme. All the herbs that were growing in our garden.

I knew we could never match Voltaire's garden in scale. He was an exceptionally wealthy man with considerable acreage. All we could hope to create would be a rustic, do-it-yourself version, not quite the formal chateau resplendent with exquisite gardens filled with topiary and statues. But gardens, no matter their size, are places where human needs and nature meet in creative and co-operative union, a point of mediation between civilisation and wilderness. Voltaire valued not just the physicality of a garden; he saw it as a valuable metaphor for how to live a life.

As I made these discoveries, one frivolous moment opened into something profound. From that moment I became captivated with Voltaire's philosophy.

The following morning, I awoke buzzing with excitement. I made a pot of coffee and found pens and scrap paper to make lists. I was determined to make Voltaire's Garden a reality. I was inflamed again, convinced I'd found the ultimate solution for us, one capable of eclipsing my recent past, making sense of our lives and doing some good in the world.

I knew I'd make it happen.

My enthusiasm was contagious. Even my twins Mary and Sarah, then just thirteen years old, responded with curiosity and interest. Our cat Pickles didn't have a say and Greg's seventeen-year-old son Jasper, who used to live with us part-time, had already moved into his mother's house to complete his schooling.

One day in the following week, when the girls left for the school bus, I called Greg in from the garden and together we started drafting budgets and sketching plans. We both thought the house should look and feel a part of the garden. Through the course of the day my Tuscan-style dream home became Greg's version of a 1930s Canberra cottage, one he felt able to build, half-clad in weatherboards, replete with dado rails, gables, architraves and finials. He wanted a U-shape building, and on that basis, I divided the interior. The U would be 5.4 metres wide, working off a standard building scale. The east wing would contain the main bedroom at the end, and a bathroom and small study off the hallway. A door in the east wall would lead outside. The girls' bedrooms would face south in the long base of the U, the other end containing a living room nine metres long. The west wing contained a dining area and kitchen situated at the end overlooking the garden. The design was simple and the U-shape created a courtyard of about seven metres square, which we would eventually enclose. An additional wing partially attached to the west wall of the main house would be for our bed and breakfast guests, replete with a deep veranda they could sit out on to enjoy the view. We kept the design simple and the dimensions as small as our needs would allow, but the final house was thirty-five squares, immense for an amateur builder like Greg. My enthusiasm held sway and my faith in him was unshakeable, even as he felt daunted by the work ahead.

Greg took time off renovating to draw up the house and site plans. By the end of the week, he'd measured, cut and nailed every stick of timber in his mind. We submitted the plans to the local council and while we waited for approval, we prepared the cottage for sale and had a dam built in the northern gully of our land.

It rained heavily not long after the earthwork, filling the dam to almost overflowing. It felt like a good omen. We sat by the dam's edge a few days later, staring into the still dark water. Greg wrapped his arm around my waist.

'It feels like it's been here forever,' I said.

'Mm.' He nuzzled my neck.

'How long it will take for the frogs and ducks to move in?'

'Not long.'

He brushed my hair from my face and kissed my cheek. I hesitated, feeling awkward. My mother's farm was right next door. She could see us from her veggie garden.

'This land is too pretty for a cattle paddock,' I said. 'I'm glad we own it. I wonder if people in the past felt the same.'

He pulled away, his gaze caught by a magpie checking out the dam. 'No doubt it's why the Catholics built their cemetery up here.'

'It's so lovely and peaceful. Our little piece of paradise. I bet the indigenous community felt the same way too.'

'The Yuin people? Probably. Although it would have looked different then.'

I looked around. 'More trees and water in the creeks. And plenty to eat. Lots of ducks.'

'They wouldn't have eaten duck, at least not black duck.'

'Why not?'

'It's their totem animal.'

'What did they eat?'

'A lot of fish probably. I know they built fish traps in the shallows of lakes to herd fish. And there are enormous shellfish middens in this area.'

'I guess they would have eaten berries too, wild cherries, wombat berries. Stuff like that. Sounds very healthy. Fish and berries. Yum.'

'Better than beef.' He stood up and reached for my hand. 'Let's go home.'

In August the council approved the plans and we put the cottage on the market. During the following months Greg worked on the site every day from dawn until dusk. He erected a steel-framed garage at the end of our imaginary driveway a few metres beyond the location of the house. Next, he gutted an old caravan we bought and turned it into a bedroom, situating it alongside the garage's north wall which faced away from the highway. He positioned at right angles to our new low-ceilinged bedroom another caravan that had been sitting in our garden. This caravan functioned as an office with high benches at each end and lots of shelves. He then enclosed the space in front of the two caravans, creating a rustic annex to serve as a kitchen and living area. Beside the annex he built the bathroom-cum-laundry using old scraps of wood left over from the renovations.

For the duration of the build Mary and Sarah would live in my parent's one-bedroom flat on their farm next door. My parents purchased the farm when they returned to Australia in 2001 after a couple of years in England, and when they also bought the land we now owned, the land that brought me back here. The girls and I had spent six months crowded into that flat, and now they would be returning. It was my mother's idea. She thought it would be helpful, especially since our finances would not cover the cost of another caravan before the cottage sold.

Through the winter months Greg laboured tirelessly, even when the icy southerlies blew, even through the spring when the dry northwesters came, even on blisteringly hot and still summer days when the flies preferred to hang out on his body, ignoring the cattle in the next paddock.

At home in the cottage, I worked furiously to complete my thesis before the house sold. It was gruelling work, abstract and other-worldly. The closer to finishing, the more I felt I'd expressed in one hundred thousand words one solitary idea – that it is far better to regard all explanations of metaphysical reality as metaphors and not as literal truths. That, and I had a lot to say about Theosophist Alice Bailey.

I submitted my thesis for examination in February 2006, my scholarship was terminated and we were on the dole as I'd feared. The only other source of income we had was a bit of cash from Greg's modelling for life drawing classes in the village. He'd stopped working as editor of The Triangle magazine – a local monthly – when renovating took over his life.

After the dignity of a teacher's salary and then a scholarship, I suffered the indignity of unemployment benefits with cheerless resolve. Finances from then on were tight. To make matters worse, we had to pretend to the government that we, or rather Greg was looking for work when he was in fact not. It came to me to write job applications for positions he was guaranteed of not getting, something I did each fortnight with grim resolve, leaving him to worry about the build.

In March we found a buyer for the cottage. The buyer adored the garden and the renovations and the sale progressed smoothly. In April we prepared to move. I was eager and apprehensive all at once, anticipating the adventure yet baulking at the thought of living in caravans on a barren hillside. Mary and Sarah shared my ambivalence. They had already endured years of upheaval, shunted from one home to another through their childhood and then one room to another during the renovations. They loved their new bedrooms and were feeling settled. It was with sullen reluctance that they began packing their books, clothes and all the paraphernalia of their teenage lives. Even our cat Pickles was concerned. She sensed the move. Every day, out of a feline fear of abandonment, she mounted the back tray of Greg's ute and sat on whatever he had piled there – old red gum fence posts, sheets of rusty corrugated iron, lengths of recycled timber, and boxes of old bottles, jars and tools.

From that moment Greg became an industrious beaver, working harder than ever to make a temporary home. But not without complaint. He'd become fond of saying, 'I don't see why we can't just live in tents.' I helped as much as I could, loading my car with boxes and bags, bringing him lunch, helping him pack up at the end of each day. But it wasn't enough. Loneliness, after months of isolation on a barren hillside, was making him miserable. He needed company, male company, with all the camaraderie that brings.

Relief came two weeks before we moved when our plumber Acko parked his ute beside the house pad's checkerboard of concrete footings. Acko was a robust man of around fifty, with thinning sandy hair and a cheeky smile. He had a property in the historic village of Tilba Tilba up the coast; a quaint cottage he'd restored. I watched from the annex window as he swung a tool belt around his waist and stuffed his mobile in his jacket pocket. He'd come to install the hot water service.

He'd also brought the hundred metres of plastic storm-water pipe we needed for the septic system. I went outside to say hello as he unloaded his ute, depositing the lengths of pipe at my feet. Then, along with his tool box, he unloaded an angle grinder, the largest and heaviest of its kind.

As Greg cornered the annex and headed over, Acko said, 'Got some homework for you, mate.'

'Homework?' Greg sounded doubtful.

'You said you were on a tight budget so I got you un-slotted pipe. I'll show you how to cut the slots.'

Acko laid a length of pipe across two saw horses and switched on the angle grinder. It jerked violently into action with a fearsome whine.

'Now watch.'

Acko cut a slot. He made it look like slicing cake. I could tell by Greg's reaction that he thought otherwise, no doubt thinking of the hundreds of slots he would need to cut.

He waited until Acko had installed the hot water service and left for the day before placing a length of pipe across the saw horses. He lifted the angle grinder and tentatively pressed the trigger. He needed all his strength to control it.

'How much does Acko weigh?' he said.

Greg weighed just fifty-seven kilos. We both knew that as he was in the habit of weighing himself every day. It had a lot to do with why I lost three dress sizes in the first months of our relationship. People can exert a powerful influence on you, just through their presence. Greg exuded thinness. Holding Acko's angle grinder, he could have done with some body ballast.

He managed to cut the slots, clutching the grinder with both hands, covering his body and face in white plastic dust. He was not wearing a mask – he never wore a mask – and he didn't stop until his hands and forearms were numb. I stood nearby, safely upwind, picturing him darting through space grimly holding onto the trigger.

I got my second taste of the magnitude of our project the day we installed the septic system. We needed a two-hundred and fifty square metre transpiration bed – a clay pad with a low clay embankment at the edges – to house the slotted pipe, which would be covered with gravel and protected by geo-textile matting, and then backfilled with soil to a depth of about half a metre.

On installation day we arrived at sunrise. Our earthmover John, a fresh-faced man sporting a tangle of thick brown hair, drove up soon after. He had a house up by the showground on the Cobargo-Bermagui Road. His family, the Evanses, had lived in the area for generations. After a brief hello and a bit of pointing and marking out, he dug the hole for the septic tank, levelled the transpiration bed and built the clay embankment. He was finished before eight.

Thank heavens that's gone! I thought, watching the first of our massive clay piles disappear. It was a short-lived hoorah. At the other end of the transpiration bed an equally massive pile of topsoil had replaced it.

As we lay the slotted pipe a tip truck arrived with the gravel. John ferried the gravel in his backhoe, where he dumped it in mounds. He dumped piles and piles of gravel on the first half of the bed, reaching as close to the centre as he could, carefully steering between the slotted pipes. In the centre, the pipes formed a T intersection and no machine could drive past this point. From there we had no option but to spread the gravel with rakes.

It was not a pleasant task. Surrounded by the rumbles and chugs of the tip truck and backhoe with the smell of diesel heavy in the air, I worked furiously alongside Acko and Greg. Raking gravel wasn't easy. The larger the gravel, the harder it was to rake. By the look of it, we'd purchased the largest-sized gravel our dump truck driver could find. I had to ram the rake into the gravel or it would glide over the surface.

'Are you okay?' Greg asked me during one of his brief but frequent pauses.

'Of course.' I said, ignoring the ache in my arms, the jarring of my wrists and the hunger in my belly.

'Then don't look so grim. It's scary.'

Scary? Me? I wasn't having fun, I couldn't say that much, but this was the kind of work that brought its own reward. I developed a rhythm. And grew a sense of pride. I conjured images of women working just as hard as me. Women in factories, in labour camps, in armies, women with heroic energy and formidable strength. Determined yes, even inspired. But scary?

At lunchtime, we took shelter from the sun in the caravan annex, a four-by-five metre space, internally clad in motley-coloured scraps of Masonite. It had a low ceiling sporting the shiny silver backing of roof blanket insulation, and a rough concrete floor. Soon to be home, but that day the annex contained just four old chairs and a picnic table. We unwrapped sandwiches and slurped coffee. I felt like a proper Aussie tradie, sharing stories of other owner-builders and their dramas, of trucks getting bogged, unfilled septic tanks floating out of their holes in heavy rain, houses collapsing before the roof went on, partially built houses swept away in a gale or razed by fire. Sitting there in the annex felt like a post-initiation scene, the new member, me, included in the ordinary life of the group. A novitiate, yes, but accepted nevertheless. I had raked and I had passed. I was all right.

After lunch the work continued. Before he connected the sewer pipe to the bathroom on the other side of the house site – a distance of about forty metres – Acko showed me how to roll out the geo-textile matting.

'By myself?' I said.

'You'll manage.'

As he walked away the wind gathered strength. Now it was certainly a two-person job. I looked around for Greg but he'd disappeared. I had no choice but to struggle along the pad length bent double, frantically trying to hold the matting in place with rocks and getting out of the way before John pulled up beside me in his back hoe and dumped another pile of fill by my feet.

John was impatient to finish. A pragmatic man, he knew that it was far less expensive for us if he did all the earthmoving in one day. Before he went home, he used his dozer to scrape a driveway. He even organized the return of the tip truck with enough road base to cover its three-hundred metre length. John then graded the road base flat. I admired the way he worked. He had an exceptional ability to shape a piece of land to best effect when preparing house and infrastructure sites. It was John who suggested we needed curves in the driveway, John who chose the best location for the transpiration bed, and John who strategically placed clay and topsoil heaps uphill for ease of relocation later.

I made sure John knew how much I appreciated his talent. It was a matter of balance. He was fond of telling locals I was the most intelligent person in the village. That made me swell. Greg was not impressed. He insisted I was mistaken, that John meant I was the most intelligent *woman* in the village. But I ignored him.

John's last task for the day was deep ripping. He used a three-tine plough to carve deep channels through the cattle-compacted earth. It took him half an hour to rip both sides of our new driveway for an avenue of trees, an area below the transpiration bed for our olive and almond groves, and a large rectangle on the eastern rise above the house site for our wood lot.

Deep ripping was an essential part of regenerating degraded land, especially Australian soils compacted by grazing and hardened by prolonged drought. Otherwise, the water ran off the slopes into gullies, filling dams and creeks but not providing much moisture for pasture. By ripping along the contours on the high points of the land, the soil was opened up and rainwater not only penetrated the rips, it also trickled underground and worked its way down the slopes, providing subterranean moisture for all the plants it met on its way. I was reminded of summer days in England, when I watched my sweet neighbour, Jo, stabbing her backyard lawn with a fork to aerate the soil compacted by the endless running back and forth of her children and mine. Here we had soil compacted by a hundred years of grazing cattle. The difference was only one of scale.

The rips, a patchwork of long weals, extended the turmoil surrounding the building site to the full width of the block. The land could breathe again, but the once smooth, grassy northern slope was now so dishevelled I couldn't fathom how we'd cope turning those long gouges into garden beds. Not for a moment did I imagine this scene as part of Voltaire's Garden. I was a fool.

Greg didn't share my concern. He thrived in garden chaos. He loved the rips; for him they held a promise of things to come, a gardening adventure on a scale neither of us had experienced before. We have both been gardeners, but of established gardens, not bare paddocks. After his course in horticulture, Greg did a stint as a gardener working in Sydney's Eastern suburbs where people had the money to afford such things. In my early twenties I spent a year vegetable gardening on some large plots and greenhouses that belonged to a manor house nestled in England's quaint Cotswolds. The owner had little interest in fresh vegetables and was happy for me and my then boyfriend to use the rich alluvial soils to grow our own food. It was the year memorable for the two hundred and fifty broccoli plants I mistakenly grew thinking they were mixed brassicas, onions the size of grapefruits strung on the backs of doors, parsnips over half a metre long, and an unbelievably abundant harvest of other produce preserved in friend's freezers around the village. It had been a source of inspiration to me ever since. But all that produce had been grown in pre-prepared garden beds. Nothing to do but bung in the seed. This, what I faced in Cobargo on those acres overlooking the most beautiful view that ever was, this was overwhelming.

And what a day it had been. At five o'clock, as the sun backlit the mountains, Greg slid his arm around my waist.

'Well done!'

'Thanks,' I said offering him an exhausted smile. 'But what will we do now?'

I pointed to the transpiration bed, taking in the rubble, clay and soil spread unevenly over the matting, the whole bed poised to become a fetid swamp when it rained. He didn't answer. We walked away looking across at the two giant heaps of topsoil on the saddle, one now sun-baked and rock solid, the other only a day old.

CHAPTER TWO

MY PLANTING FRENZY

'Please send me everything you can in the way of flowers and vegetables. The garden was completely bare; we must start from scratch...'

VOLTAIRE, *VOLTAIRE IN EXILE.*

I t was a one-hundred metre walk from my mother's house to the annex, taking the shortcut through a farm gate and past the granite outcrop. The girls slept in the flat and spent most of their spare time in the annex, now cluttered with our possessions.

On entry to the annex, the door to the left led to the office caravan. On the opposite wall was the door to the bedroom caravan. Between those two doors we'd put one of our sofas. Mary's piano sat against the bedroom caravan wall and on the other side was a tall bookshelf stuffed with books. Below the window in the west-facing wall we'd positioned an old gas cooker – the oven sat beside the gas rings – on a makeshift bench. There was enough room at the end of the bench for a small square chopping board. Below the window on the north-facing wall Greg had erected a low melamine bench which I used to collect the dirty dishes in plastic tubs. There was no running water in the annex. In its centre sat Greg's old oak table on a thick woollen rug. There was little floor space remaining.

I soon found spare time to be with my children didn't amount to much and I hardly saw them. The first Monday after we moved, they arrived at seven for breakfast and left half an hour later for the school bus. Looking out the annex window I watched them walk to the gate, Sarah small and blonde, Mary tall with long red hair. An unlikely pair, they barely looked like sisters. Uniformed head-to-toe in navy blue, backpacks bulging on their backs, for all their adolescent defiance – they were fourteen now – they were still my babies. I was unexpectedly overwhelmed, my mind awash with memories of when they were young and cute, and I wanted to rush out and hug them. But I couldn't give way to the maternal longing in my heart. I had work to do.

Greg had been heaving slabs of broken concrete – urbanite, he called it – from the pile over by the garage since dawn to cover the clay pad outside the annex. I dearly wanted him to start on the house piers but winter was closing in and the clay was turning to mud. We'd laid out pallets as grillage but we were still tracking in mud so he made the crazy paving a priority.

He enjoyed puzzling out shapes and laying them in place. His resourcefulness and practical know-how gave him the confidence to build, but his real passion lay in breathing life back into the old, the discarded, the unloved. In the era of the plastic, ready-made throw-away, a man like Greg had no place.

His soul was retro, it pulled him into a past that pre-dated his own lifetime.

Laying crazy paving was heavy work and I had no part in it. I headed down to the rain water tank to join the huge cluster of potted plants fanning across another clay pad. All last summer Greg had collected seeds and cuttings from out cottage garden. He struck grevillias, lilli pillis, abelias and wattles, mulberry trees and hazelnuts, enough lavenders to create a hedge, and rosemary, marjoram, tarragon and thyme. He propagated ground covers, lifted snowdrops, day lilies, naked ladies, tulips and gladioli. No plant escaped his notice. Now they were here, hundreds of them all gathered together in a huddle by the rainwater tank, I faced a choice, water each and every pot daily or get planting.

The deep rips were the only places where the ground was pre-dug. I loaded a wheelbarrow with my trowel and ten native seedlings – hakeas, wattles, tea trees, banksias, and bottle brushes – and headed past the annex and garage to the rips on the south side of the saddle.

Past the rips the land arced downward to a small dam, rising again to meet the highway. I paused as I always did when up on that land, taking a moment to gaze at the rooftops of Cobargo. A working village, with gift shops and art galleries to satisfy tourists, and a post office, supermarket, newsagent, agricultural co-op, butcher, baker, doctor, pharmacist and vet all catering for the local community. Cobargo boasted an accountant, an upholsterer, and a mechanic. The only business to leave the village was the bank. Beyond the village the hills rolled on, and then there were the mountains of Wadbilliga National Park. I breathed in deeply, as if sucking in the beauty. It was one of those views that made me feel bigger than I was.

When I turned to look around at the deep rips and the building site I felt myself shrinking. The longer I left those rips, the worse they would become. The weeds would take hold and I'd be battling with kikuyu grass runners. There was only one way to turn the jumbled mess I saw into what I wanted to see, a burgeoning garden. I kneeled down and grabbed my trowel.

The soil was damp and loose. I pushed the full length of my trowel into the ground with ease. The weeds relinquished their grip on the soil without a fight. It was not long before I'd dug and weeded ten little patches, planting a baby native in each one. I found it so easy that when finished I went back to the pots and chose another ten. Then out of the weeds I created twenty small circles of protection. The trees and shrub seedlings were tiny, almost invisible set in their weed-mulch defences. The rips looked set to swallow them up. I named my planting the Infirmary and went to fetch a watering can.

By midday the sun streamed through the north-facing window, warming the annex. I turned on the radio and hailed Greg who was ramming sand between concrete slabs with a cold chisel. We ate cheese sandwiches and drank coffee listening to Radio National.

'A severe drought and growing food shortages in Ethiopia?' I said in response to the news item of the day. 'It'll turn into a famine soon enough.'

'Sounds like Ethiopia needs to get its house in order,' he said, reaching for his cup.

Every nation needed to get its house in order. I didn't say it. Instead I said, 'Famine is a problem for all humanity.'

'That's just rhetoric.'

'How can you say that? This famine could be worse than back in the days of Band Aid thanks to the changing climate.'

'And did all that aid make a difference? No.'

I could feel myself getting irritated. He could be contentious at times. And Africa was close to my heart. I took a breath.

'Then what do we do? Pretend it isn't happening?'

'It's a sick world. What people need to do is what we're doing here. Set an example.'

'And barricade ourselves in to fend off the climate refugees.'

'I didn't make the world the way it is.' He took another bite of his sandwich.

I didn't want to bicker with him any longer. 'The crazy paving is looking great,' I said with forced cheer, getting up to put my cup in one of the plastic tubs.

'Thanks,' he said, draining his cup and heading back outside with what was left of his lunch.

Later, in the afternoon's long shadows, I stood by the Infirmary and waited for the school bus. I was keen to involve the girls. I wanted them to feel a part of the project. I thought if I nabbed them before they reached the annex they might be persuaded to help.

Past the Infirmary where all my little babies looked perky, the driveway followed a boundary fence two-hundred metres to the entrance gate. Two heads appeared bobbing along and then the whole of Mary and Sarah as they ambled down the driveway. I had a full three-minute wait for them to reach where I stood.

'Hey, girls,' I said when they were in earshot. 'Look.' I pointed at the triumph of my day.

'Looks great, mum,' Mary said with a quick glance.

Neither of them showed any indication of stopping. Deflated, I followed them inside.

Sarah dumped her school bag on the table and opened the fridge.

'Can I use the Internet?'

'For homework?'

She took that to mean yes and opened the office caravan door.

'What's for dinner?' Mary said.

'Soup. But first I want your help.'

'Now?' She sounded incredulous.

'It won't take long.'

I handed her a pair of overalls.

She stared at me. I waited, holding her gaze. She put the overalls on.

'I'll grab the tools.'

I loaded the barrow with plants and headed up the drive. Mary sauntered behind me to the gate.

'What are we doing?' she said as I parked the barrow at the end of the rips.

'Planting a row of wattles and pepper trees from here back to the plants by the garage.'

'How many will that take?'

'We'll have to pace it out. Four giant steps between each one.'

I handed Mary my trowel and grabbed the gardening fork.

'I'll loosen the soil. You can do the planting.'

I dug over a spot and stood back. Mary swept her long red hair from her face. She needed a hat but wouldn't wear one. She freed the area of weeds and made a small hole. Then she took a pot, turned it over with the base of the plant stem positioned between her fingers and with a half turn plopped it in the hole. After backfilling with her trowel, she patted the ground. She was a natural. I made a little reservoir, watered in the baby tree and then mulched with upturned weeds. Together we worked our way down the rips.

On my way back from filling the watering cans, I managed to drag Sarah away from Facebook, but she didn't share Mary's willingness to help. She trudged up the driveway, stopping halfway to stroke Pickles who'd flopped at her feet.

'Hey, Sarah,' I called back to her. 'Would you fetch us some more water?'

'No.'

'Then will you weed?'

'No.'

Not taking no for an answer, when she had at last reached our outdoor workstation I handed her a wattle and prepared a hole.

She yanked the wattle out of the pot by its leaves, severing half the roots, leaving a little root ball attached to the wattle. I was aghast.

'Have a care.'

'It's just a stupid plant.'

She threw down the trowel and stomped back to the annex. In my mind, she'd been sacked.

It took Mary and I two afternoons to plant fifty trees along one side of the driveway. While she was at school I planted a row of gum trees on the other side and staked them with tree guards. In years to come the trees would form a magnificent avenue. Now all I saw from the annex window were green plastic sleeves.

Cobargo nestles in a giant amphitheatre. The mountains of the Great Dividing Range extend their reach to the coast in two arms, one to the north and one to the south of the village. In winter, misty air pushes inland on the ocean breeze and rolls up the rivers and along the valley floors until, trapped by the mountains, it blankets Cobargo in mist and fog, making early mornings a visual delight, reminiscent of oriental landscape paintings.

One cold morning in June, when Cobargo snuggled under a soft, white blanket and the rounded top of the forested hill behind was visible above the mist, I stood on the crazy paving clasping a mug of coffee in both hands and gazed in wonder. To the right of the hill and beyond the village, green pastures edged with shrubs and trees rose towards the horizon, flanked on the other side by Murrabrine Mountain and the ranges of Wadbilliga; thirty-four thousand hectares of pristine wilderness where rivers had carved deep gorges and the terrain was mostly inaccessible. The Bega Valley's secret.

Beyond the annex, Greg was wrestling with the urbanite. He'd finished the crazy paving and made a path from the annex to the garage. Now he was doing some terracing. Massive slabs of urbanite were leaning against each other like half-fallen standing stones. He manoeuvred a slab into a space he'd dug along the house-cut batter, several metres from the edge of the paving.

'Watch your back,' I said, not wanting an injury to slow the build.

'It's okay, as long as I don't let it fall,' he said, catching his breath. 'I doubt I could lift it up again.'

Greg took a sort of boyish pleasure in turning the concrete slabs into instant terrace walls. In a matter of hours, the deep cut at the corner of the house became three garden beds, each one five metres long. I was right there with my trowel and a wheelbarrow full of pots. I planted an apricot tree, two native pea bushes, convolvulus, garlic chives, daisies and a clump of dwarf dahlias. Greg looked on in amazement.

'You don't have a plan, then?'

'I'd rather just get the plants in the ground.'

'I suppose we can move them later.'

'Move them!' I managed not to raise my voice too much.

Greg shrugged and walked away.

Planting was compulsive. I knew I wouldn't be satisfied until every pot was empty. Besides, there was little else to do. We were waiting on the timber to start building the sub-floor of the house. I'd ordered the timber in April from a local spot miller. Close to three months had passed. I was getting more worried every day. The delay meant more time in the confines of the caravans. More time missing the company of my girls. 'Any day now,' the miller said whenever I phoned him. Any day now was fast taking on a different meaning: never.

Greg didn't share my anxiety. 'No point worrying over things beyond our control,' he said over breakfast one morning.

'But what will you do?'

'The next thing.'

He still needed to build the house piers. Pallets of concrete blocks had been sitting there all month. I knew my parents were eyeing the slow progress and wondering how long their generous invitation to have the girls would go on.

The next thing turned out to be the vegetable terraces. Last year we flattened a top terrace out of the humps of topsoil our earth-mover John had dumped in long rows – soil from the site cuts. The second and third terraces were still a mess of weed-tangled humps.

We were standing out on the crazy paving. Greg grabbed the fork and rake leaning against my wheelbarrow and headed down the hill, passing the house cut with its rows and rows of concrete pads, and past the rainwater tank resting on a bed of sand on clay. Sand fringed with large-stoned gravel, held in place by a ring of stones about a foot high. Greg's handiwork. The tank was flanked on three sides by clay batters, as if it were a huge can in the lap of a giant armchair. Beyond the tank sat a two-metre mountain of clay. On the rise above the clay sat a second tank filled with dam water. Greg had dug a trench and buried poly pipe all the way to the main tank, where he'd installed a garden tap. The water was gravity fed and flowed fast when the tank was full.

I followed Greg down to the rainwater tank and stood beside the swathe of pots that filled the area between the tank and the top terrace. From there, I watched Greg, knee-high in weeds, stabbing a hump with a fork. Apart from the bay tree I'd planted last spring at the terrace edge near the house site, the top terrace was a sweep of bare ground. At my feet were rows and rows of herbs. Without hesitation I took two pots of rosemary to accompany the bay tree. Working my way along the batter-edge of the terrace, in went herb upon herb. Hyssop, tarragon, garlic chives and marigolds soon surrounded the bay tree. Where the terrace fattened towards the middle of its length, I planted marjoram, sage, thyme, lemon balm, more tarragon and echinacea. When I reached the narrow end of the terrace below the clay monolith, I turned back and filled up the space with liquorice root and more rosemary, along with French sorrel, salad burnet and onion chives. Ignoring an ache developing in my lower back and the hunger in the belly, I planted rows of leeks and asparagus, and on the back edge near the rainwater tank, a lavender hedge. In two hours, I'd just about filled up the whole terrace.

I glanced down at Greg who was still flattening humps. Spurred on by his relentless capacity for hard labour, I found space between some tarragon and garlic chives, raked a bed and sowed turnip seeds. I watered in the seed and stood back, satisfied.

Greg saw I'd stopped working. He thrust his fork into his freshly raked soil. 'Need some help?'

'I've done it,' I said, grinning at him.

He cast a critical eye along the length of the terrace. 'So I see.'

'Aren't you impressed?'

'Sure.'

I didn't quite believe him.

He joined me on the top terrace, scanned my haphazard planting once more and took the rake from my hand.

'There's room just here for a bed of carrots.'

He pointed at a bare patch of ground in front of the marjoram. With meticulous care he marked out a long straight rectangle following the terrace edge. He raked the soil smooth, raised the edges to stop water run-off, sprinkled on carrot seed and covered the bed in river sand.

I cast my eyes back over my turnip bed with dismay. I'd made a rhombus of lumpy uneven soil. But that's the price you pay for wanting things done as fast as possible.

Voltaire's Garden, with its grand and noble connotations, was a powerful force compelling me want to make our land worthy of the name. I was affected, too, by the beautiful views all around us, wanting a garden that blended and merged into the landscape in a seamless whole.

Greg had the same fiery will, doing the work of ten, never resting as long as the sun shone. But something else was driving him and I couldn't work out what that was.

I went back to the annex and sat down at the end of the rustic pew Greg had found at a garage sale. The late-afternoon sun dipped below the mountains and the sky, cloudless and clear, turned magenta. I gazed into the distance unexpectedly overwhelmed by a longing for Africa.

There was nothing in the landscape to trigger the emotion. Nothing in the darkening sky. Nothing in my immediate surroundings to remind me of my time in Ghana. But the loss of my role in the Ghana link affected me strongly from time to time. It was a sort of grief. By now the Pampawie garden would be flourishing. I wondered if it looked how I imagined it, all shady and lush, with ripening mangoes and pineapples. I wondered if I would come to terms with the crazy sense that somehow, I had to atone for leaving, a gnawing need to prove to myself at every turn that it had been the right thing to do, knowing I could only do that when I felt in my heart that I'd replaced it with something worthwhile. Even my doctoral thesis, examined, approved and praised, didn't fill the void. That day I'd left England for Australia, I must have left hope behind too. And it was crazy – four years had passed. I had to make Voltaire's Garden my homage to Pampawie or I was doomed to live in perpetual remorse and I'd become as bitter as a gherkin.

I went into the annex, switched on the radio to Classic FM and made soup, chopping leeks and potatoes on the small, square chopping board – an off-cut of bench top leftover from Greg's cottage. While I waited for the soup to cook, I took up my knitting, a bulky Aran cardigan of bright red, with enough detail in the pattern to absorb me through the long, winter evenings. Two rows later the door swung open and Sarah and Mary, who'd gone up to the flat to get changed, dumped their homework on the bench under the window.

I took pleasure in their presence. I asked them about their day. We chatted.

When it was too dark to work outside, Greg appeared, grabbed some clean clothes and took himself off for a shower. Night closed in and the soup proved filling. Conversation was light. Leaving the washing up until the morning, we all settled into our usual routine, Sarah in the office on the computer, Greg lying on our bed reading a book, me on the sofa, knitting, and Mary on the piano practicing her dark chords. Mary was having piano lessons in Narooma every other Saturday, which was when I did a grocery shop, but her interest in death and black metal meant the only classical music she cared to play was Beethoven. Thankfully, she tired soon enough and once the keyboard lid was down, on went Classic FM.

My planting frenzy continued. July, and it was time to plant fruit trees. One lunchtime, before Greg took off outside I suggested we write a list. In ten minutes, we were heading down to the Cobargo Co-op to place an order for oranges, lemons and limes, plums, apples and pears, and pecans, almonds and olives to accompany our mulberry, peach and apricot trees, stone pines and hazelnuts. The fruit and nut trees would arrive later as bare-rooted stock, but the olives and citrus were ready to take home. We loaded them into my city-dweller's hatchback now turned carthorse, a real country car with muddy streaks, a dusty dashboard and grit.

At home, I admired the olives, hoping they would be enough to fulfil our annual consumption of olive oil. Of the many varieties, I selected those suited to local conditions and best for pressing, mostly Verdale and Corregiola. I wanted my olive oil cold-pressed, green and fruity. The supreme replacement for butter. Whenever I thought of my very own cold-pressed olive oil drizzled on wholemeal toast topped with slices of homegrown tomato, I all but swooned.

I loaded the olives into a wheelbarrow and headed for the rips by the dam. It was already three o'clock. Soon it would be time to cook, but I knew planting in the rips would be quick. As I headed back to the car for another load Greg's son Jasper swung a smart white car into our driveway. He beamed a smile as he pulled up beside me. He'd just got his driver's license and had come to celebrate. He was half grown up and half a kid still, his trousers hanging off his hips, his sandy hair in surfie dreads. Pickles sauntered over to say hello, flopping down at Jasper's feet for a tummy rub. Greg joined us, suggesting cups of tea and biscuits, and it was beginning to look like an afternoon off, but I was having none of it. Not now I had a willing helper in front of me. Jasper had always made himself useful and he had, I hoped, grown out of his habit of working painfully slowly.

'There'll be no such thing as a free lunch at Voltaire's Garden,' I said. 'It'll be olives, then tea, in that order.'

Greg and Jasper exchanged good-humoured glances and Jasper shrugged.

We planted the olives in under an hour, using buckets of worm castings and a mix of blood and bone and lime to boost the soil. I worried about rabbits and ring barking, so we enclosed them with circles of chicken wire. And since we wanted to harvest our olives, when it came time we'd probably net them. It was tedious and expensive but necessary. All our fruit trees would need the same treatment to protect them from parrots, flying foxes and rabbits. I imagined our garden a few years on, an ocean of ripening produce housed inside vast enclosures, a tent city of wire and nets.

Afterwards, as we sat around the table in the annex over tea and cake, Jasper announced he would soon be leaving Australia to spend a year in London. We wished him well but we would miss his willing, if occasional help.

A week later my mother passed a message through the girls to say she'd pop down for a visit that morning. Living next door, she could witness our progress as it unfolded and she often popped in. She took a keen interest, pleased I had at last settled in Cobargo, a village she adored.

When she came to Cobargo in 1980 to visit her own mother, she loved the area so much she stayed. I followed six months later. I was nineteen then and full of post-punk adrenalin, high on the music that was coming out of Britain and the exciting cultural outpourings of 1980s England and New York. I had Talking Heads and U2 fever. I yearned to see Echo and the Bunnymen and Bauhaus, play dress ups and go to parties. I wanted to have unmitigated fun. Australia had appeared to me then a cultural desert, and with my jaundiced Londoner attitude, Cobargo was its crassly inane epicentre.

At that time Cobargo was traditionally rural, its population of several hundred comprising mostly the old farming families, like the Tarlintons. A migratory wave of 1970s hippies had by 1981 either disappeared into the hinterland going completely bush – many rumoured to have grown acres and acres of marijuana – or left preferring the warmer climate of Byron Bay on New South Wales' north coast. Those who remained seemed to have become absorbed by the landscape, integrating seamlessly into the local population. From my myopic perspective, the cultural situation was intolerably dull. I didn't stay.

At twenty-eight I returned, this time an emaciated waif escaping a relationship turned sour and the seedy underworld life I had lived in London and Lanzarote, a Canary Island off the coast of Morocco. I looked haggard. I managed to enter Australia with a one-way ticket from Bali on a holiday visa, something I am told is unheard of. Cobargo was still a sleepy little place full of run-down weatherboard cottages and vacant house blocks. This time, I made an effort to fit in. I got a job cleaning motel rooms. I found a boyfriend. He didn't last. I left again after another six months and went to live in Perth.

The third time I returned it was 1995 and Mary and Sarah were four years old. It was my great escape from their father, precipitating a torturous passage through the courts. Cobargo was kind to us and my perspective changed. I got to know people. I stayed for a full eighteen months, leaving because my internal horizons were wider than the sky, my aspirations reaching beyond the mountains.

When I came back in 2002 I was suffering burnout. I might have thought I was fine, but I wasn't; I was a shambles. My confidence and self-esteem were at their lowest. I felt a complete failure and while I had the tenacity to build a new life, I missed the old one badly. I still did.

Unlike me, Cobargo underwent a renaissance in my absence. Dilapidated weatherboard houses had been renovated, and the main streetscape had trees and a stylish footpath. Coffee was no longer instant. Tree-changers had bought up five-acre subdivisions previously owned by dairy farmers, experimenting with organic gardening, permaculture and biodynamics. Some kept bees, some an orchard, others worms or snails.

Sometimes it takes years to appreciate a place. At first, I was trapped in an attitude of cultural superiority, then my heart closed due to a confusion of negative associations, blocked by personal values unsuited to the place. Village life is not for everyone. So I came and I went. This time, I had joined the ranks of writers, musicians, artists and nature lovers, drawn for the same reasons away from urban living. This time, Cobargo was my exile. I was staying. Perhaps I would find here enough creative inspiration to become part of its literary cohort, alongside Arthur Upfield, Zane Grey and Olga Masters, who had all resided in the area at one time or another.

Now we were living on the land, I aligned myself with Voltaire, whose outspoken belief in liberty, both the cause and the result of his own spells in prison for upsetting the French Regent, led him into exile. He spent the last twenty years of his life banished from Paris for his critical views of the *ancient régime,* and escaping, too, the wrath of his once close friend, King Frederick II of Prussia, by whom he felt betrayed. Exile was another edge, a frontier, a state of not belonging, a suspension, an escape, somewhere safe, somewhere known or unknown, different, and entirely suitable for someone like me.

My mother appeared in the doorway of the annex as Greg and I were drinking tea. Her white, curly hair was windswept, her cheeks rosy. She was a slim and attractive woman of fair complexion, and quintessentially English in manner in a refined and cautious kind of way. She looked a little nervous as she poked her head in, not wanting to interrupt.

I beckoned her in.

'We were expecting you.'

Greg drained his mug and after a brief exchange of pleasantries and a polite apology, he escaped through the door.

I went and put the kettle on.

'I made a fruitcake.'

'I can smell it.'

We settled down to tea and cake and she relaxed. She'd been more anxious than anyone to see the timber arrive. She was more edgy every time I saw her. Things hadn't been easy ever since my stepfather Bryan – a retired marine engineer with a happy-go-lucky if cheekily stubborn attitude and a wide range of practical skills – had offered to help Greg in any way he could and Greg flatly refused the offer. Offended, Bryan never stepped foot on the land again.

This time I had news that I knew would make Mum feel better.

'We've bought an old caravan for the girls.'

'They're okay at mine,' she said a little too quickly. She didn't mean it. Two moody teenagers tramping about month after month, love them as she did it was not ideal, not in the long term.

'We both know this build is going to drag on and on.'

She was slow to respond.

'Greg?'

'Yep.'

'It won't be much longer and you'll be rid of them, Mum,' I teased.

'Oh, they're no trouble. Really.'

'The caravan will be delivered next week and then Greg can renovate it. It needs a bit of work. But they should be out of your hair by the school holidays – that's only a couple of weeks away. Okay?'

Clearly it was. Besides, I couldn't wait to have the girls here with me, where they belonged.

While I sipped my tea, she took an interest in the pamphlets on woodlots and coppicing strewn across the table. We needed a woodlot to be self-sufficient in firewood. We planned to use the deep rips behind the garage. They would meet the stand of red and apple gums on the granite outcrop and we'd left a wide path between the rips to make easy access up to my parents' farm. The trees would need to grow for several years before they could be coppiced for firewood so naturally I was keen to see them planted this winter.

Mum placed a newspaper cutting on the table. 'I came over to show you this. I found it the local paper. You might be eligible.'

It was an article about another small-holding, two keen gardeners and a Landcare grant for native regeneration. Landcare aimed to restore the native forests clear felled in the region during the 1960s and 70s. Almost all the old-growth forest had gone, the only remaining pockets found in inaccessible places, including the gorges, gullies and ridges in Wadbilliga.

After my mother left I reached for the phone to call our former neighbour and Landcare coordinator Dave, who rented the house on the corner of our old street when we were renovating. Dave and his partner Debra were Masters graduates in Social Ecology, having studied in the same school at the University of Western Sydney where I undertook my PhD. We became instant friends the day we met.

A few days later Dave pulled up in Landcare's Toyota Hilux – a huge, white monster of a ute, high off the ground. Peering out from inside the annex, I thought to myself that maybe he should have arrived on a bicycle in light of his profession, but Australia, like Africa, was vast and the terrain often rough.

Dave was a welcome presence. He was tall and big-boned, with a mop of dark hair framing a kind and wholesome face. Other than my mother we had barely seen a soul since we moved here, and there were days, cold, wintry days, when I felt very lonely on that exposed hillside. Besides, he loved to support any project that involved the regeneration of the land. He, above anyone we knew, took our wildly ambitious idea of Voltaire's Garden seriously. He drove up on occasion, always appreciative of our achievements and he took a keen interest in the way we were doing things.

I went outside as Greg exited the garage. Leaving them to chat, I went back into the warmth. Moments later they both entered the annex, Dave with a bunch of forms in hand. He guided us through them. Not only could we receive government funding for trees, he told us, but also for fencing them off from any grazing stock we planned to have.

Before he left we took him on a site tour. It was good to walk and talk and wave our hands around expansively, showing him the newly levelled section of the second terrace and the planting of herbs on the terrace above, then heading down to the dam and back around the bottom edge of the transpiration bed where the olive grove would be, telling him of all our plans. It was hard to let him go. But he had a job to do. The moment his Hilux was making its way down our driveway, I made a start on the application.

Dave returned a few days later, walking up our drive one late-July afternoon with his three-year-old daughter Ruby on his shoulders. He came with a smile and a cheque for over two thousand dollars, and the paperwork.

He looked tired. In the annex he slumped in the sofa, cuddling Ruby, whose huge doe-like eyes followed me around the room. I found her a picture book.

'Tea?'

'Nah. Gotta get back. Deb's cooking. Smells good in here, Isobel. What've you been up to?'

'A curry. Lamb and lentil.'

'Meaty. I guess you people need it, with all the work you're doing. The place is looking fantastic already.'

'Do you think so? It's hard work, as you know.'

'But you are outside, in the fresh air. I wish I was.'

'I thought in your job you would be out and about a lot.'

'I would be, but for the admin. Which reminds me, make sure you keep a log of how many hours you put in.'

Thousands, I thought as he left. It's sure to be thousands.

The next day I phoned an order through to the Co-op for a hundred trees for the wood lot, choosing Blue Box and Southern Mahogany, which were native to the region and made excellent fuel.

Outside, I found Greg digging up self-seeded wattles and red gums around the dam. Scores of seedlings sat in chunky clods of earth.

'You've been busy.'

'Might as well. They're another resource. We can't leave them here anyway.'

'I'll help.' I went back to the annex for my gloves.

Only, I didn't return. On my way up the hill I decided to

squeeze in a few domestic chores. Dishes needed drying, clothes folding, and rubbish taking to the bin. As usual I was in a self-imposed rush. In the laundry, I leapt onto the raised platform that housed the shower to grab a towel. Greg had had the crazy idea of building a split-level laundry-cum-bathroom, with the washing machine and trough on a concrete slab and the bathroom area raised up about half a metre. Beneath that area was the water pump. Ingenious, he thought at the time.

Greg had still to make proper stairs, so we usually made do with a small table as a single step. Today, the table was elsewhere. As I turned around, I forgot about the drop and leapt back down in a single stride.

Moments later I felt a twinge in my rear. Soon a searing pain gripped my whole left buttock, radiating from a locus of deep pain near my hip. I gasped, limped to the annex and eased myself into a chair. I felt nauseous. I couldn't move. My gluteus maximus had gone into spasm, or so I thought. Damn! I was struck down like Job, thwarted just as I had begun to improve my strength.

A short while later, Greg poked his head in to find out where I'd disappeared to, and seeing me in pain, asked if he could do anything. When I told him I didn't think so, he promptly left the annex and headed back to the dam. No tea and sympathy there then. I rested and eased my way around the annex feeling miserable, caged, a prisoner held captive by gripping pain.

I decided not to bother the doctor, after all, it was obvious to me that I'd hurt a muscle and I didn't fancy my local GP probing my posterior. And I decided not to phone my mum, because she would have told me to see the doctor.

The following morning, in spite of the pain, I could endure the captivity no longer. I took my sore buttock for a walk to the dam and found Greg loading baby red gums into a wheelbarrow.

'If you take them up there I'll plant them,' I offered.

'Are you sure?' A look of concern appeared in his face.

'I don't see a choice.'

He didn't argue. Ever since we embarked on the project we'd got locked into the same mindset. It wasn't quite grim determination, but it wasn't all joy and lollipops either.

I headed back up the hill, gathered some tools, and limped my way over to the rips. A dull, deep ache throbbed with every step. At the top, when I put down the barrow and turned around, the pain in my rear gave way to appreciation as a mellow winter sunrise bathed the western mountains in soft pink, highlighting Dumpling Ridge and Mount Dumpling against the cool blue background of the ranges behind, defining the gullies and ridgelines, accentuating the depth of field.

As always, I was spellbound. Every location on that land afforded a subtly different outlook and there where I stood, the view was enchanting. I imagined myself in a rotunda, painting landscapes. I thought of all the people I would invite to the place when it was built and how enthralled they'd be. I would make scones with home-made jam and a nice pot of tea and we would sit together and admire the tremendous view.

A sharp pain and the arrival of Greg reminded me I had work to do. It was the same process: dig, weed, plant, water, mulch and guard. Only now I worked through every stage in searing agony, my buttock deciding to squeeze itself into a tight knot, and every move I made seemed to make it squeeze tighter. I managed to plant fifteen trees before retiring to the annex to lie on my side.

In the days that followed, I refused to be crippled by my uncooperative behind. Each morning after the girls had gone to school I planted more trees, first our volunteers, and next the ones we'd ordered. While I was planting the woodlot rips, Greg took our four-stroke push mower designed for the suburban backyard to the gully above the dam. I could hear the old mower and see him between the trees wading through knee-deep grass. He was mulch making.

It did seem crazy to mow acres of cattle paddock with a backyard, four-stroke push mower, in fact it *was* crazy, but the end result was worth it – heaps and heaps of paddock clippings mixed with rotted cow poo. Greg was a mulch enthusiast, believing it to be the most essential ingredient for improving Australian soils. Grass mulch, like any other mulch (gravel, woodchips, bark), protected the earth from drying out and suppressed the weeds, but it had an additional benefit, grass mulch also made soil. Worms, slaters and crickets munched their way through, gradually transforming it into the organic matter the soil craved.

With the trees planted I mustered the will to help. I grabbed a small grass rake, left the building site behind, and walked through the soft grasses under the canopy of red gums below the granite outcrop. It was mid-afternoon and the sun was low. Shafts of soft light beamed through creamy, mottled trunks. The distant mountains turned smoky-grey violet. Our tiny patch of open forest evoked images of parkland scenes on jigsaw boxes. I paused to absorb a moment of stillness while Greg re-fuelled the mower.

For the unfit and inexperienced, raking acres of paddock clippings was arduous work. My injured buttock rebelled with every reach and pull of the rake, my arms ached after a minute and I soon felt like giving up. Bending to collect armfuls of mulch to cram into the old wool bale he'd unpacked for the purpose was excruciating. But my will overrode the pain and I genuflected before the nearest mulch pile and then the wool bale.

Seeing my face screwed up in pain, Greg killed the mower to help.

'Do what you can, Isobel. Stop when you need to.'

I heard him, but I also knew he needed me to work alongside him. He felt as overwhelmed by the scale of things as I did. It was hard for either of us to be indulgent with each other, and comfort and sympathy was not his way. He said he cared and I knew he did, but he was too busy to show it.

To keep our spirits up when we felt low, we clung to our vision, we reminded ourselves of the values it represented and how important those values were to us. We both felt driven by something far deeper than personal concerns. Perhaps we were tapping into a current of energy that pulsed through Voltaire, Thoreau and the Romantics, and was today affecting scores of like-minded people across the globe. But then, wasn't what we were doing something natural, what human beings have always done, farmed, gardened, tilled the soil in various ways? Until the industrial revolution turned our collective attention elsewhere, to man-made things, and money. I was not one for stripping off our consumerist garb and wallowing in nature like a band of merry hedonists, but I did believe that we could do both, look both ways, and more than this, we had to. Which was why I so admired roof gardens on city buildings, community gardens, English allotments, and people who dug up their lawns to make way for the vegie patch.

Threats to human and planetary survival were motivating people to return to a gardening connection with nature, if only to secure their own food, but the current that flowed through our veins was not fear or insecurity, it was ineffable, simply there. It was as if something was stirring in humanity's soul and there at Voltaire's Garden we were tapping into it.

I took a short break, leaned on my fork and surveyed our block. The garden was a swathe of tree guards; the green plastic sleeves were neatly arranged in rows in the woodlot above the annex, in a staggered formation in the infirmary between the garage and the western end of the front garden, in two neat rows along the driveway and randomly arranged in the olive rips below the orchard. It looked from a distance like we were growing plastic, not foliage, and when Greg's mother Carolyn visited last week, she'd thought they were gravestones. She was getting old.

Greg fired up the mower for one last attack on the long and lush grass around the natural spring that fed our dam. Moments later, the mower sputtered, emitted a loud bang and died. He fiddled with the throttle and yanked the starter cord a few times to no avail. The lawn mower had declared itself defunct.

'It was old,' he said with some sadness.

We raked up the rest of the clippings and dragged the wool bale and the mower back up to the garage, leaving mounds of rakings for later collection.

Undeterred and yet again ignoring the pallets of concrete blocks waiting to be turned into house piers, Greg started another mammoth project, this time levelling the sodden area around the septic tank to create a space for the girls' caravan, using the surplus soil to backfill the transpiration bed, which had remained a two-hundred and fifty square metre bog since April. A few days later, satisfied with his efforts, he proceeded to tackle the arduous task of backfilling the transpiration bed itself, taking a wheelbarrow to one of the two huge piles of topsoil in front of the house site.

He managed to fill a tenth of the area when the girls' caravan arrived, in considerable disrepair. We positioned the van – a beast of a thing – on the sculpted land Greg had prepared. He planned to spend the following fortnight renovating it. The moment the caravan was in location, he began gutting the interior. I looked at the transpiration bed, and then at the piles of soil. The distances weren't too great and the barrowing was downhill. I was definitely stronger than I was when we moved there, even with my painful behind. It was with an air of fatalism that I took over as barrow-girl and, ignoring the nagging pain in my buttock, I shovelled, barrowed and raked, back and forth past the caravan on and off all day.

I did the same thing every day until both piles had almost disappeared and the bed was full. I even began to enjoy it.

One day I saw my mother walking towards the transpiration bed where I was raking out my recent soil dump. As she neared I stopped and waved.

'Come to help?'

She laughed nervously. I leaned on my rake and observed her. She was still nervous. A few bonks from the caravan and her eyes darted in that direction. Greg didn't appear.

'I have some news for you,' she said.

I thought perhaps Bryan was ill or there had been some disaster. But no.

'We put the farm on the market yesterday.'

'You're selling?'

I felt a little queasy. The whole idea of Voltaire's Garden was suddenly under threat. Who would my parents be replaced by? I couldn't mask my disappointment. I enjoyed having them close.

'It's Bryan's back,' she said. 'He can't do all the heavy work.'

My stepfather had spinal problems from an injury he incurred years earlier, resulting in two back operations, neither of which went terribly well.

'I suspected as much,' I said, letting her off the hook somewhat for not discussing this with me before. It was not like my mum to be so secretive.

'What made you think that?' she said.

'When I used your computer for Internet banking, real estate sites came up in the search. I could see from the history you'd visited them recently. Sorry, I didn't mean to pry.'

'And you're not upset?'

'Not at all,' I lied, wanting to reassure her.

'It won't be for a while. We've got to find a buyer.'

I leaned my rake against the wheelbarrow. 'Come on, let's have tea.'

She followed me back to the annex.

I wondered if they'd ever settle. For a long time, I had fixed in my mind that my mother was the sole reason I came back to Cobargo, leaving my home, teaching career, the Ghana Link, family and friends. And now she was on the move again. Where would she move to this time? Timbuktu?

I knew in an instant that thought was unfair. Besides, my problems in England began long before my parents had decided to return to Australia, the result of work overload and the stresses of single motherhood, but when she left there was a gaping hole in my life that nobody around me could fill. She flew back to Australia the day the Twin Towers fell, and despite my efforts I had no one to look after Mary and Sarah for all the occasions when my professional life required my time. I knew, too, that I no longer had enough energy for the Ghana Link, which in the near future would demand even more of me and I was already finding it hard. Sarah was missing her grandmother terribly and fell into a childhood depression. I had to contend with workplace bullying from resentful staff members, a nasty consequence of my own career success at the school.

To add to my woes, one spring day my entire backyard fence fell down in a storm. It seemed an apt mirror for my life. I felt I had reached a brink. If I continued in the same vein I was sure to collapse like my fence in the next wind.

It wasn't just the lack of motherly support and workplace and domestic stress that caused me to leave England. I had a powerful urge to get away, right away, from the filthy air that hung over the countryside, from the crazy busy-ness of consumption that led to endless queues and congestion, from the superficial, self-centred values that seemed to have enshrouded much of the British populace concerned more with computer technologies than their own communities, and from the insane Christmas and annual holiday hype that ran up credit card debt for all but the most cautious. England, it seemed to me, had gone barking-mad. As my paternal grandmother old Ma Grimble would say, 'It's giving me the screamin' ab dabs'. It was not the England I knew and loved back in the 1980s; it was nothing like the life I led in Oxford as a student and the hilarious times I had living in a London squat. My England then was filled with optimism and adventure, drinking beer in old English pubs and cycling to the markets to buy vegetables.

Driving back from the shops in the smog during the Easter break and trying to imagine achieving a healthy, sustainable, clean way of life in England I had little sense that it was possible. I knew there were cleaner places there, but they couldn't compete with the lush, wild, rain forests of Ghana, with Africa, a continent close to my heart, let alone the two Australian idylls in my imagination, one inspired by Peter Carey's *Bliss*, the other by my old friend Julia Hillam's family farm in Coonalpyn, a village south of Adelaide in South Australia.

I was eleven when I knew her and spent many weekends on her farm, absorbing the life her mother, father and sisters led. The farm ran merino sheep and I remember the fleeces her mother spun and wove into rugs scattered throughout the farmhouse. They had a milking cow, chickens and ducks, and they were intensely self-reliant, even making their own soap. It was a formative time for me, and I'd carried the experience close to my heart ever since. It was in the same year I read Hesba Fay Brinsmead's *Pastures of the Blue Crane*, a lovely story about a young girl who underwent a sea change when she finished boarding school in Melbourne and resided with a grandfather she barely knew in a run-down shack in the country. She despised the change at first, but eventually embraced her grandfather, the shack and the new life she found.

On my return from the shops, I switched on the computer to check emails and I stared at the computer background Sarah had selected last week, a real-estate photo of a parcel of land on a new subdivision adjoining the farm my parents had purchased upon their return to Cobargo. I knew it was bait, my mother's promise to bequeath it to my daughters a manifest manipulation, if genuinely felt at the time. When she suggested that I could build a house on that land, in spite of myself I began to succumb to her maternal scheming, and I started to embrace the idea, with trepidation, yes, and with excitement.

I walked to the kitchen window to see if Jo next door was around. Seeing her head bowed over her kitchen sink, something I could not have done before the fence blew down, I waved. She didn't look up so I walked over and knocked on her back door.

'Hey, Jo. Are you busy?' I asked, entering her kitchen as I had done every day for months. She was my confidant and personal advisor, and I was hers. She was a feisty woman with four young children and she had an intense passion for home decorating. Her house dripped with colour and fabric, so homey and inviting. Jo was earthy and we talked candidly about everything. She'd lost her mother to cancer shortly before

I moved in, and I guess I replaced that hole a little, but I felt more like an older sister.

After a long, long chat over tea, as she was sneaking a cigarette when her kids weren't looking, she implored me to leave.

'Isobel, for heaven's sake, what on earth would you want to stay here for? I'd give anything to be in your shoes. Go girl, just go. Do it. Think of the sunshine, the land, the ocean, all that space.'

I stared at her. She meant it. And because she did and she was the closest friend I had, I listened to her. I decided, in spite of all my misgivings about returning to Cobargo, and all that I would be leaving behind, to take up my mother's offer. The land represented peace, health, well-being and, knowing Cobargo, a self-imposed exile.

The decision had not been easy. I liked my home, a little terraced house, with its Victorian fireplaces and pocket-handkerchief garden overlooking woodland. I liked to stand at my upstairs window and gaze across the plains of Leicestershire, imagining the Battle of Bosworth, or a young George Fox, founder of the Quakers, growing up in the nearby village of Fenny Drayton or, a short distance on, the notorious highwayman, Dick Turpin sheltering in The Cock inn. So much human history, just there beneath my gaze, a view marred by the pinkish haze on the horizon.

Cobargo offered a safe place to bring up my daughters, and a relaxed and wholesome lifestyle. Jo was right.

CHAPTER THREE

ONE WOMAN, ONE PADDOCK, ONE DROUGHT

'All's for the best in the best of all possible worlds'

DR PANGLOSS, *CANDIDE*

Every time I acted impetuously I told myself afterwards it had to be my last impetuous act. That I must curb my impulsive nature. I would resolve to measure and reflect and make all my decisions carefully. And then I acted impetuously all over again. Even when I managed to convince myself I'd given due thought to a situation I found on reflection I'd done no such thing. It's only with hindsight that I could see the passion colouring my musings, bending them out of shape like light through a prism. I moved in with Greg having known him a full six months. Plenty of time to find him compatible. Or so I thought. Far longer than my previous leaps of love. Which was true. And nowhere near long enough to really know him. As I was finding out.

I awoke one November morning to hear the north wind rattling the annex door. Feeling despondent in the face of another day of hot dry weather, I got up and made coffee on the stove. Greg appeared wrapped in a towel and hurried to the bedroom caravan as the girls appeared, dressed for school. I must have overslept.

As the girls chatted and busied themselves with breakfast, I leaned against the bench, waiting for the coffee pot to hiss. Greg exited the bedroom in his usual work gear, caught my gaze and indicated with a tilt of his hand that he'd take his coffee outside. I found him on the pew stroking Pickles when I went out to hand him his cup.

Inside, I watched my daughters as they slurped through their cereal then turned my gaze to the window. I was emotionally parched like the land I saw outside; we were both craving respite from the spring winds and the endless sunshine that had turned verdant pasture fallow, and the soil anhydrous since I finished planting in July.

The whole of New South Wales was in drought and a blanket of weather anxiety seemed to hover over farms and towns across the state. Water was life, without it, death's shadow loomed all too close. Plants shrivelled, trees died, livestock were culled, dams were drying up, town water supplies were threatened and at Voltaire's Garden I had hundreds of baby plants to keep alive. Weeds were not an issue. There were no weeds. Nothing grew. The ground was so dry when I pounded it with a crow bar I could hear an echo.

After the girls headed off for the school bus, I got showered and dressed, went outside and took a watering can to the one garden tap. I was instantly reminded of the one solitary village pump in Pampawie, my garden tap servicing an entire community of plants.

The early morning sun was burning my skin and when

another gust of wind whooshed past, whistling through the wizened carrot tops, I sighed and returned to the annex.

The fly-screen door slammed shut behind me. I swung the main door shut as well to keep out the heat, then I looked over at the clock and sighed again. Eight-thirty, and I was trapped inside a five by four metre box crowded with furniture, with its shiny, silver ceiling and multi-coloured walls, in the heat.

A bound copy of my doctoral thesis had arrived by post the day before and it sat all formal looking in the centre of the table. I had been commended by all three examiners for originality and bravery. All well and good but in my current circumstances the award meant very little. I picked it up and put it on a high shelf in the office caravan.

What next?

Pickles lazed on the pew and Greg was building. He began on Father's Day after our timber miller, Charlie, arrived with the first delivery in late August – we'd finally given up on the other guy when he told us he could only supply half our needs – and it was then Greg finally set to and built the piers.

Charlie was a local miller, his timber of fine quality with few twists and bows. Greg said Charlie was a bushie who really knew his wood. He loved to be out on his own with his dogs in the forests around here. He cut firewood, milled anything from tomato stakes to massive beams, and occasionally took on a job like ours.

Charlie's timber came just in time. After three months working on the garden, Greg had become fidgety. In his search for things to do he'd built a rustic post and rail fence out of old red gum posts to edge the parking bay outside our imaginary house, along with a gravel and brick path leading to where we thought the front door of the house would be. It was strange to see something looking a hundred years old next to a hundred and five concrete pads. It was as if there had been some terrible fire or wind, and we were re-building a home razed to the ground or swept away by a hurricane. It looked even more bizarre after I planted up the edges of the path with abelia cuttings for a hedge.

Bursting with pent-up energy, once the piers were built he took to Charlie's timber like a man possessed. He sawed, planed, chiselled and hammered all day, and the next. In two weeks, he had built the sub-floor. Then he turned his attention to framing the house. He made tremendous progress. In another few weeks, the frames for the walls stood proud and true. He even notched each wall stud into the top and bottom plates to help prevent twisting, a practice rarely seen these days because most frames were built from radiata pine, not unseasoned hardwood.

How he managed to build in the heat and the fierce sun was beyond me. My fair English skin burned so quickly and after ten minutes in the sun I always felt dizzy and sick.

That November day, the radio announced a high of thirty-eight degrees. For me that meant hours spent inside with a book and a fan.

Our books were crammed in piles filling the one tall bookcase that took up the back corner of the annex, the rest lying in random heaps in the office caravan, filling all its shelving and much of the space under the benches. I browsed through the bookcase, pulling each pile of books towards me and tilting my head to the side to scan the titles. When my neck objected to the tilt, I reached for the top book of the next pile. To my surprise and delight it was Voltaire's satirical novella, *Candide*.

I settled down on the sofa wedged between the two caravan doors. I thought it about time I read the story that had inspired our build, and began with the introduction.

Voltaire wrote *Candide* in 1758 after the catastrophic

Lisbon earthquake of 1755, which killed fifty thousand people. At the time, the French and Spanish Inquisitions were continuing to persecute heretics of the Catholic Church. Europe was in a state of political upheaval. Then German philosopher Leibniz, along with Alexander Pope and Jacques Rousseau, chose this moment in global history to promote a system of philosophical thought called Optimism. It was a philosophy that incensed Voltaire. Based on the notion of an all-knowing, all-powerful God, proponents of Optimism denied the existence of evil and in doing so, swept away death, suffering and wrong-doing in morally suspect arguments, including the Catholic government's explanation of the cause of the Lisbon earthquake. Proponents of Optimism claimed it was a divine judgment, one that then required a series of ghastly public executions.

In *Candide* Voltaire sums up their view through Candide's tutor, Dr Pangloss, whose absurdly Optimistic phrase 'All's for the best in the best of all possible worlds' is the catch-phrase of the book. Pangloss – pan, as in all, and gloss, as in a superficial and misleading explanation – uses it to rationalise every dreadful situation Candide encounters.

I'd heard similar arguments proposed by some New Age acquaintances. Somehow, all the bad that happens in a life is 'what brought you to this point'. As if I had to go through all *that* in order to be here now. Good grief! I could not fathom how anyone could think that a human death toll from an earthquake was a good thing. Nor could I condone the notion that human suffering resulting from human action was in any way good. 'All's for the best in the best of all possible worlds' seemed to me a contrivance, a compulsion to permanently wear a smile, a happy hat, always interpreting the world and its events and circumstances as necessary for some greater good, and dismissing suffering as therefore somehow necessary.

I hadn't got through many pages when the door opened and Greg stepped inside. His face shone and I could smell his sweat from two metres away. He groaned.

'Can I get you anything?'

'No. I'm okay. I have a water bottle. I just need the house plans,' he said, opening the office caravan door.

'While you're here, listen to this,' I called to him through the caravan wall, re-opening the book and reading the first page.

'Candide sounds like us,' Greg called back, 'two ignorant, blindly optimistic fools embarking on a project the size of Everest.'

He was right. We both felt the strain, the project too huge and we knew we had barely begun. For months we'd been working seven days a week, rising at four and not stopping until dusk. Our goal was similar to Candide's, to find or create an environment in which we would be happy and fulfilled. And, like Candide, we'd encountered and would no doubt continue to encounter many difficulties and hardships along the way.

Perhaps encountering hardship and suffering was the lot of all philosophical fools who ventured forth to discover happiness. Perhaps the idea of the goal in the philosopher's head blinds her to the difficulties in reaching it. Or was it more the case that wisdom is gained through learning things the hard way?

There seemed to me many Candide types in Australia, a country where land was in abundance. From the original shacks built by the early settlers, like the one we renovated, through to projects like ours, men and women had struggled hard for months and years to build themselves a home, a lifestyle and a garden. It was a tradition, to build a home on a block of bush, to enjoy the natural environment, the beauty. To inhale the scent of eucalyptus.

And the drought was nothing new either. When I returned to Australia in May 2002 with the intention of building on this very land, Cobargo was in the grip of a drought that didn't break till the following February. It was during the drought when I met Greg.

By then I'd been waiting six months squashed into the two rooms of my parents' flat, with the girls and the furniture brought over from England. Beds, wardrobes, tables, chairs and boxes had taken over most of the floor space, and while school life consumed much of the girls' week, I spent my days crowded out by clutter, feeling more and more oppressed. To make matters worse, I had trouble fitting in to village life. Every time I ventured out – which was not that often – whether to buy something, check the mail, or attend a folk festival soiree, I was compared to my sister, Michele, who migrated with my parents in 1980, married a dairy farmer, had six children and had lived in the area all her adult life. It was as though I had no authentic identity of my own.

After many monotonous weeks, I began to ask myself if I had done the right thing. My heart ached for Pampawie and Agnes and all the promise of the Ghana Link. My life seemed to have collapsed like the twin towers the day my mother came back here. Her timing was incredible. She could not have picked a better moment to rip away the only supporting structure holding up my life – her. That day when I watched in horror the towers collapsing on the staff room television, two blazing infernos and panic on the streets, I could have had no idea that a similar thing was brewing inside me.

I tried to fit into Cobargo but by November, I felt like a prisoner, trapped by circumstances. Impatient to get on with my life, I relinquished the notion of building on the land and bought a little house in the village instead. It was a small, Hardiplank kit home on the edge of the village, a charmless, rectangular box with low ceilings, large, almost-square windows and a tiny non-functional kitchen, a place for first-home owners, struggling families and single parents downsizing after the property settlement. It had no character, unlike the quaint, old weatherboard houses nearby, with finials on gables, double-hung windows and latticed verandas. Even the rustic, mud-brick houses in Pampawie with their gutter-less, corrugated-iron roofs and rammed earth floors had more appeal. I was determined to do something with the house to make it more palatable, more congruent with me. A house, I decided, was like a dog, it should match its owner. Only, the house and I did match, we were both demoralised, empty shells looking for new life.

Exacerbating my malaise, the sun rose every day in a cloudless sky and hot, drying north-westerlies replaced the harsh, winter frosts. While I waited to move into my box of a house, I felt as dry as a desert, burnt out and thirsty. I was listless and dissatisfied. I didn't come halfway round the world to be bored.

After exhausting my small collection of unpacked novels, I searched for something stimulating in the second-hand bookstore in the village, and found a cheap copy of *Candide*. One afternoon I read the first chapter, only three pages long, but I was soon disheartened by the romance about to blossom between Candide and Cunegonde, so I read no further, snapping the book shut, feeling like an old spinster.

I'd been a single mum for about a decade. My life was wasting away when I could have enjoyed a partner, a husband. My face was still attractive, my brown hair showing little grey, but my eyes looked haunted and I had put on too much weight. The jeans I told myself my mother had been shrinking in the wash for the six months I'd been living at hers had stayed the same; I had grown instead. I looked like a frump.

That afternoon, Mary and Sarah arrived home from school full of excitement. They loved going to school in Cobargo. They got to wear sweat shirts and track pants instead of white blouses and ties. They had made a ton of friends. The kids were much friendlier and the teachers less strict. With only around a hundred kids on the role, the school was not intimidating; it had an intimate, wholesome feel, where individual creativity was valued as highly as academic success. To me it felt like a state-run community school compared to the formal feel of schools in England. It was a great relief to see the girls so happy. They could run around freely; there was so much space, so much outdoors fun to have.

I'd promised to take the girls to a village concert, a fundraiser at the School of Arts Hall. I was not exactly in the mood for fun, but forced myself anyway, throwing on a skirt with an elasticated waist and a snug mauve top, telling myself I'd better suck in my tummy for the next few hours even if it made me faint.

I stood in the queue outside the hall to pay, watching the girls as they ran towards their friends. They were eleven years old and their differences were more striking than ever: Mary, a tall, thin redhead, Sarah, small, blonde and cute.

Soon they were lost in the crowd.

I read a promotional flier while I waited and discovered what I was attending: A fundraiser held by The Crossing Land Education Trust, established in 1998 on a beautiful parcel of land on the Bermagui River some twenty kilometres to the east of Cobargo. The event boasted scores of musicians performing well into the night. I read that The Crossing focused on educating youth in the ways of sustainability, permaculture, renewable energy, grey water recycling, re-using old materials and carbon storage in local forests. It was so named because the trust took young people on journeys from snow to sea, traversing the many different types of native forest between the Snowy Mountains, down the escarpment of the Great Dividing Range to Bermagui on the coast. They travelled by bike, boot and boat. It seemed a very worthy cause and a welcome alternative to the usual trivia nights, sausage sizzles and Friday nights at the pub I never went to.

The event was well-attended; when I entered the hall, it was packed. A motley sea of heads moved below windows set high in walls of Baltic-pine lining boards. A fan in the barn-style ceiling far above made a half-hearted effort to circulate the warm late-spring air. I had never seen so many people in Cobargo. They must have come from all over. I spotted many familiar faces from the village including the owners of the newsagency, some former neighbours of mine, and some artists and builders and staff from the primary school. And I spied some members of the Agricultural Show Society committee who I had come to know quite well as I was then the secretary, a position I acquired when I arrived in Cobargo last May.

That was my mother's idea. Both her and my grandmother were former show secretaries. Mum thought it would help me fit back in and in a way it did. I liked the role and the local farming community.

When I first came to Cobargo in 1981 at the tender age of nineteen, I was befriended by an affectionate group of grandfathers who went to the pub for the chook raffle on a Friday: Bluey, Donny, Bill, Clemmy and my stepfather's best mate Claude, who found me a good darts companion. The men adopted me as one of their own. They had all passed away and Cobargo had changed and grown, but the down-to-earth rural vibe remained. The way I knew the village, it was always friendly but fairly divided, historically through religious tensions between families, and more recently between the locals and the 'greenies', 'hippies' and other blow-ins, all classed as outsiders. I guessed people would always have their preferences, but the social divisions were no longer so strong that they couldn't be transcended for events like this.

In the hall the familiar faces of Cobargo blended well with the scores of bearded bushies and women with long hair and flowing dresses looking very New Age. It didn't seem to matter how anyone dressed. Looking around I even spotted a punk man in leather, sporting a brightly coloured Mohawk.

Alone, I gravitated towards Christine and John Quelch, a mature couple from the show society committee. A flirtatious mood came upon me, a feeling that I had nothing to lose and everything to gain by casting around for eligible men. Convinced as I was after ten years of single life that there could be no male soul to match me anywhere on the planet, it didn't prevent me being a tease.

After exchanging greetings, I cast my eyes around, turned to John and said, 'All I see are mothers and babies, why don't you introduce me to the available men?'

To my astonishment John obliged, steering me towards a small man with close-shaven, fair hair, a lean body and a quirky smile: my first candidate. I sucked my tummy in tight as we headed over, dodging the others mingling about.

'Greg,' John said, catching the man's attention. 'This is Isobel'.

Greg gave me a thespian bow and said, 'Pleased to meet you.'

'Greg's editor of the local magazine. The Triangle,' John said, taking his new role a tad too seriously. 'And Isobel here is secretary of the show society.'

With that, John walked away and left us standing together, neither of us knowing what to say. Greg seemed about to head off. Not wanting to lose the opportunity, Greg being the first single and attractive man I had met in a very long time, I said, 'What do you do, besides editing the local rag?'

'I'm a philosopher.' He said it with much seriousness but there was a sparkle in his eye.

'Me too,' I blurted, wondering what had compelled me to say that. I felt pretentious, not having got past page three of *Candide* in all the months since I'd arrived in Cobargo.

Worse followed.

'What school of philosophical thought are you into?' I said.

'Well, specifically I guess I'm a phenomenologist,' He was taking me seriously and it was unnerving.

'Me too,' I said again. What was I saying! I winced. Had I blown it? And what on earth was a phenomenologist?

We grinned at each other. Two self-described philosophers living in Cobargo – what were the chances?

We exchanged telephone numbers. His ended in 247, mine in 248. A sign? Surely not. But that was how we both took it. I saw it in his eyes.

The interaction lasted only a minute. He disappeared into the crowd and I continued on my playful quest, escorted by my ambassador, who steered me towards his second choice, another small man, a lawyer this time, quite shy, the sparkle of wit seemingly absent from his eye. A very brief and awkward exchange took place upon which my conspirator, by now enthusiastic, pointed across the room to a taller, bald headed man with rounded features and a certain air of arrogance, or perhaps desperation. I shook my head, declining an introduction. Something about him warned me off. After that, I tired of the game and sought the company of other people I knew in the room tossing up my duo of potential suitors, with the numbers 247 and 248 rattling around in my head. It was not a hard decision. The numbers won.

. . .

From the comfort of the sofa and the relative cool of the annex I observed Greg, who had exited the caravan with the house plans.

'Can I be of any help?' I said. He only needed me when he needed to raise a frame.

'Afraid not.'

He left the annex and I pictured him out there on the subfloor in the searing heat, all lithe and tanned, spending yet another day chiselling wall studs. He must be lonely. And here I was hiding from the heat, wondering if he had chosen the right woman for the project. I had all the ideas, I was good at that, but what about the skills to go with them? Wouldn't he have been better off with a robust woman with practical building and landscaping skills? A woman capable of cutting timber, a woman fearless of power tools, who could measure, and cut a straight line. A woman who could take the heat. Greg often told me how useful I was, how it was me who maintained the steady focus, me who as site manager organised orders and deliveries. I laboured for him too, helping to pack up tools and move timber, but still, it didn't seem enough.

Right then I had only one major task and it felt enormous. I had to keep my baby plants alive come what may. I had to be pragmatic and stoic, not the soft, city dwelling westerner I once was, accustomed to modern conveniences, like running water in a hose. I was a peasant now, a poor farmer relying on muscle and simple technology – like a bucket.

While I waited for the day to cool enough to get outside and water, I made coffee in a saucepan on Greg's old gas cooker as I listened to Classic FM, the one radio station we had all agreed to like, and then reclined on the sofa and returned to *Candide* to ride out the worst of the heat.

The following day the weather was much the same. It was Saturday. Before the morning warmed I filled two twenty-litre buckets and two watering-cans and put the lot in the wheelbarrow to water the trees along the driveway. It was too far to carry water by hand and the idea of using a barrel filled with water loaded on the back of the ute – a strategy Dave had suggested – couldn't be implemented as Greg had requisitioned the ute as a mobile tool shed, parking it a few metres from the building site.

I kept the barrow steady to ease the sloshing as I walked. Any bump and water swirled and spilled. With a careful eye on the terrain ahead, I navigated my way through the building site and onto the driveway, steering the barrow on the smoothest course I could see, wondering what Cobargo thought of me in my baggy white gardening clothes, a wide-brimmed hat and fly veil, trekking the three hundred metres to the gate.

Once there, I slowly worked my way down the driveway, giving each plant only the smallest amount of water, a half a litre if it was lucky, carefully drizzling the water down to the roots and nowhere else. The buckets filled the watering cans and the barrow filled the buckets until there was no water left. My lower back ached, my shoulders and arms strained, and I felt twinges in my left buttock.

It took two trips and one hour to water the driveway plants, hidden in their tree guards surrounded by dying weeds and the knobbly clods of earth in the rips. In a week I would need to repeat the process. More plants needed water but it was seven o'clock, already hot and I wilted like a delicate flower in need of shade and cool air so I retreated to the annex.

Mary walked in looking flushed.

'You're up early,' I said.

'I got too hot.'

'Not surprised. It must be stifling in your caravan. Did you leave a window open last night?'

'What window, Mum?'

I cringed. She was right. That caravan was very light on ventilation. To prevent leaks Greg had nailed shut most of the windows and covered over others with cladding. He'd even built a second roof over the original, to keep the rain out. One end of the caravan was sectioned off and had enough space for a single bed and not much else. Mary had a king single at one end of the main space and the other end was filled with her piano and a small sofa which we'd managed to force through the narrow door. For the last few months anyone in the annex was no longer forced to endure her dark chords. Since then, though, she'd progressed to *Moonlight Sonata*.

A northwester kicked up dust on the paving outside. Pickles pressed her nose against a Perspex panel Greg had put in the wall above the office caravan. She liked to shelter between the caravan roof and the protective canopy he'd built when he enclosed the caravans. Sarah entered the annex and slammed the door behind her, exclaiming that her bedroom had become a sauna. Only Greg remained in the sun, nailing noggins between the wall studs. Incredible. The weather was punishing, we could have been living on the salt plains of Ethiopia where the fire winds blew, not here in a region noted for its verdant pastures and annual flooding rains, the rains that hadn't come since I'd arrived with the girls four years earlier.

That November of 2002, when I was still living at my parents, the girls and I helped clear their paddocks of cow dung to rejuvenate the pasture. We called it 'sodding', a euphemistic term for hand-picking dry cow pats to expose the soft grass beneath, loading the pats on a trailer and dumping them in heaps on granite outcrops. The dry northwester would gust, flies latched on to faces, heads and backs and sweat trickled down armpits. I felt ill in minutes. But we had to do it. By then, my parents were hand-feeding their cows and there was so little rainwater in their tanks; for months I had to do hand wash clothes in the girls' bathwater, and toilets were rarely flushed.

I was relieved to move into my Hardiplank box in town – at least it had running water – until December gave way to January and the hot weather intensified and became insufferable. The house faced southwest with little shade to protect it. When the temperature rose above forty, I would lie on my back, naked but for a sarong, watching daytime television without interest. I rose only for water and food, each time with a head spin.

On cooler days I prepared for the annual agricultural show in February. As secretary I had articles to write for the local media, and it was this that brought me back in contact with Greg. As editor of The Triangle, he received the copy. He worked from home, so I called by.

He lived just two blocks away, but I drove as my legs felt too weak to make the distance. I parked on the verge and entered a lichgate covered in wisteria. An uneven dirt path led to the deep, cool-looking veranda of a rundown cottage, cluttered with pots, boots and an old hat stand. I noticed a lean, tanned, muscular man in a blue singlet and large sunhat forking the ground, and melted. It was Greg.

Noticing me, he turned and smiled. 'Welcome,' he said in a mildly theatrical manner typical of him.

'I have some copy for The Triangle.'

I felt so nervous I was shaking. I handed him the copy and turned to go home with a hurried goodbye.

'You must come round for coffee sometime,' he said to my back.

Did he mean it? I turned.

'Yes, that would be nice.'

Providence was on my side. Another committee, Cobargo's

primary school P&C, wanted someone, me, to drop by Greg's with copy.

Several brief visits and phone calls later, and his 'you must come round for coffee sometime' turned into 'come round tomorrow at ten.'

The following day, on the dot of ten, I entered the lichgate. Again, he was working in the garden.

'Let's go in.'

He rested his garden fork against the trunk of an old camellia.

We walked down the path between herb and cottage garden beds, under the veranda past the pots, boots and hat stand and through an old fly screen door, entering another veranda, this time closed in, with an old linoleum floor, painted weatherboards and casement windows leading onto rooms that had become internal. This veranda was deep and full of old furniture. A door at the end led through to his kitchen.

'Have a seat.' He gestured towards a chair.

I sat at the old oak table in the centre of the room while he made coffee. An old kitchenette stood in one corner. The bench under the window was crowded with appliances and beside it was a gas stove. An enormous brick chimney dominated the east wall and an old sink piled high with dishes was crammed into the corner facing the window. He placed two coffee cups on the oak table.

'How do you take it, black, white, sugar?'

I told him. 'What a lovely place you have here,' I added politely, reminded of the grotty student rentals I'd lived in.

'Thank you,' he said. 'Needs a lot of work. I've drawn up plans. Want to take a look?'

He went and fetched them, unfurling a roll of paper and spreading it across the table and leaning over me as he talked me through his ideas.

As he spoke I felt myself sinking. I was captivated. I blushed and my palms sweated. I crossed and uncrossed my legs. I leaned forward and then I leaned back, not knowing what to do with my body. My mind raced. Could he not see how agitated I was? After two hours I could no longer endure my own nervousness and took my leave.

I spent the following weeks consumed by infatuation. We saw each other every day, Greg visiting and charming me with stories of his life. He won over Mary and Sarah too, gaining their approval, something they didn't readily give, having placed themselves like Rottweilers between me and all potential suitors ever since I left their father.

When alone, I pined for Greg, as if I were sixteen and in love for the first time. I needed a distraction, and I found one.

Mary and Sarah had needed swimming lessons for years and Cobargo had its own pool. Through the hot summer weeks, we walked to the pool every day. The rest of Cobargo seemed to have had the same idea, the pool always crowded with kids, mums and dads, in the water, lying on towels, sitting under the pavilion or paddling in the baby pool. In my heightened state it felt like a luxury resort.

The girls loved the cool water. They learned to swim thanks to Jim, the weather-beaten ex-surfie turned pool manager and swimming instructor, known locally as 'Jim-at-the-pool'. I could think of no one better to teach my girls and, it seemed, neither could any other mother in the area. He'd probably taught every kid at the local school, freely offering instructions and advice, and he worked a twelve-hour shift seven days a week for the whole six-month pool season. People like Jim made Cobargo a special place to be, they bound the small community in profound and benevolent ways. Every Cobargo needed a Jim or two.

While the girls swam, I hung out with Jim and several

mothers, some of them friends – sweet, country women, married for decades and settled in their own lives. They shared in the flush of my new love, as day by day my affections grew. I beamed, I glowed, I started to lose weight and I walked on air.

To my surprise, I stayed in the clutches of love's intoxications, and for once my feelings were reciprocated. We shared a groove of understanding like a pair of chickpeas in a pod. Greg was the father of three boys: Aiden, in his twenties and living near Sydney; Jasper, fifteen and living with Greg part time; and Jasper's younger brother Ali, who lived with his mother. Mary and Sarah didn't seem to mind Jasper, who didn't seem to mind them, and no one seemed to mind either Greg or I, so it was easy to see a future in the romance.

There were other members of our families to consider. While step children might skirt around eyeing each other off warily they would, eventually, smile, nod or say hello. Not so with cats.

The moment I purchased my little house, I acquired Pickles, a beautiful kitten, a cute ball of tortoiseshell fur, her tail pointing straight up, the sign of a good mouser.

Greg had Rose and Rose was an old cat, nearly as old as Jasper. Greg had cared for her nearly all her life. She was a tawny tabby with a hauteur that came from years of pampering and indulgence. Rose – who passed away before we moved to Voltaire's Garden – was territorial. She had seen off several dogs in her time with a lightning swipe of her paw. Old age had made her slow, but she could still put up a good fight.

Romance blossomed to the sound of purring and many days spent on Greg's porch, swinging back and forth gently on the wooden seat he made for his mother and then kept for himself, admiring camellia blossoms, roses and daisies surviving the summer sun and the dry.

Our relationship deepened the day I told Greg that my

little house needed a kitchen renovation and a new patio and I couldn't afford a builder. Greg was keen to impress. He offered to do the work himself, so we agree an hourly rate and I bought the building supplies.

He arrived one January morning, backing his old ute into my garden, the back tray loaded with tools and timber.

'Hi, Isobel.' His silky voice softened my heart.

'Where will you start?' I asked, watching him unload tools.

'When I work that out I'll tell you.'

'Coffee?'

'Lovely.'

He worked long and hard, transforming my kitchen from a dingy confused little room into an open, clean and stylish one. I was impressed. When I spent a week in early February in a tin hut at the showground taking entries for the upcoming show, he built me a patio. What more could I want in a man? He had brains and brawn and tremendous versatility. I was even more impressed when he spent the money he earned on power tools for his own renovations.

On the last day of the show it rained and the entire Cobargo community was relieved. Dams fill, grass greened and lawn mowers were soon busy after months of inaction.

I stood in front of the fan, watching the girls eat breakfast at the old oak table that took up most of the floor space in the annex, wishing it would rain. The dam's water level was half a metre below full capacity, the water lost through evaporation in the heat and the drying winds. The drought was making me pessimistic and I'd started to wonder if it would ever rain again, and how long our dam water would last if it didn't. I found myself identifying with every parched plant and thirsty animal, every struggling farmer across the drought-stricken land.

Through the annex window I looked up to the sky, my eyes imploring 'please rain' to a solitary cotton tuft of cloud.

The drought was blowing dust into my imagination. I considered buying cacti, or dropping everything in favour of a job in an air-conditioned office in the city. Where was my oracle foretelling good fortune? Where was hope? When would the drought end? Would it end? One thing was certain, hope wouldn't be found on the bureau of meteorology's website. Every day I checked for rain, only to be informed that it would be dry. I read 'chance of a shower', and muttered 'a rat's chance in hell of a shower', because the showers didn't come, not over us, anyway.

After weeks of watering for hours morning and night my endurance waned: I needed help. I recalled the two teenaged girls I'd met in Ghana, who fetched water from the village pump for their mother each morning before school, water they carried in large metal bowls they carried on their heads. No doubt they would rather have been doing something else.

My girls were now strong, healthy fifteen-year-olds. I hoped they had not become too consumed by Western youth culture not to care. Mary would surely be willing after her impressive planting last June, but Sarah was not the cooperative type.

They stood to put their cereal bowls in with the washing up. Seizing the moment, I said, 'Girls, I have a job for you.' I crossed my fingers. 'Will you please help me with the watering?'

'What? Now? Isn't it too hot?' Mary replied, with an imperious toss of her red hair.

'No, not now. And not just once. I was thinking every day after school.'

'Okay,' she said slowly. 'But you'll have to tell us where.'

Sarah was silent.

'What about you?'

'Do we have to?'

'If you don't, then Greg will have to help. It's too much for one person. I honestly don't think I can take much more, my back is sore, my arms hurt, my...'

'Mum,' Sarah cut in, 'We'll do it. Mary already said so.'

Ah, the united voice of twins.

'I'll draw up a watering chart.'

They surprised me. Each day after school and on weekends, the girls watered a section of the garden. On Mondays they bucketed water from the dam for the orchard of twelve fruit trees, each a metre tall, standing in a bed of unevenly raked earth at the end of the transpiration bed. I assigned the strawberries behind the tank – three score of them mulched with newspaper, cardboard, bark and weeds – for Tuesdays and Fridays. It took at least ten watering cans but the strawberry patch was thankfully close to the tap. On Tuesdays they also watered the citrus trees, requiring a can full each. Wednesday was harder because the watering was uphill - the infirmary and the stone pines, mulberry trees and a row of plants behind the garage. Thursdays was 'wood lot right' and Fridays 'wood lot left'. I'd divided the wood lot into two sections due to its size. It was up on the eastern rise. On those days I ferried the water halfway in buckets, ignoring the dull ache in my left buttock that seemed to be a permanent fixture whenever I carried anything.

I designated the olives in the rips below the orchard and the twenty tea trees scattered around the girls' caravan for Saturday. The hardest watering day was Sunday. The abelias and grevillias outside the front of the house site were easy enough, but then there was the driveway. All this, every day for weeks, they did assiduously and without complaint.

Keeping the garden alive was not the only worry. At its peak last winter, our twenty-thousand-gallon rainwater tank had reached only a third of its capacity and after months with no rain, we risked running out of water. The egg timer had been in the shower for weeks and now we caught the run off from the shower, which I used for cleaning. We bucketed dam water from the solitary garden tap to pour into the toilet cistern.

One day, tired of carrying buckets of water for the toilet, a task I alone had inherited, I had a bright idea. I would collect the washing machine water to pour into the cistern instead. It seemed a practical, labour-saving thing to do, in spite of the six or seven buckets full of brown, fetid-looking water that cluttered the laundry-bathroom on washing days. Practical that was, until a putrid smell started to permeate the space.

At first, I wasn't sure where the smell was coming from. I cautiously sniffed the outflows in the shower, laundry trough and toilet bowl, but smelling nothing, I approached the cistern.

One small sniff was enough. I reeled back, clenching my nose, and exited the room. The cistern, or rather some 'thing' in it, was rank.

I inhaled deeply and crept back inside as if the cistern-thing might have grown legs or wings, and cautiously took a look. Beneath the murky washing water, I discovered a strange, primitive life form, a congealed mass of brownish-grey slime. Trying not to heave, I seized the toilet brush and plunged in my bare right arm.

Grey-water recycling was a little more involved than I'd thought. I removed my arm, deposited the primitive thing in the toilet bowl and reached for the bleach.

But wait. What was I thinking? You couldn't pour bleach into a septic system. I put the bleach back and scrubbed out the cistern instead.

My triumph in water conservation involved the washing up. I developed a way of washing dishes in little more than a puddle. It was by no means easy. I had to cart the dirty dishes in plastic bowls from the annex to the laundry. There I collated the wash-up into degrees of dirtiness until surrounded by a swathe of crockery, cutlery and pans, ready for the puddle wash. For rinsing I drew one cup of hot water, which I carefully poured from glass to cup, from cup to bowl, and from bowl to saucepan, dunking utensils along the way, managing to rinse the lot in that single cup of water. It had to be a record.

I was proud of my water-saving abilities, but they were hard work and I was developing a preference for one-pot meals. I began to wonder why we couldn't shovel food into our mouths with spoons from a communal pot. I tried not to hate it, but the reality was I loathed washing up that way; not only was it tedious, with all the bending and reaching my back seared by the end of it.

Washing, cleaning, watering, cooking, drinking, all seemed to need so much water and the burden built until I weathered the drought like a curse, with absolutely no sense of humour whatsoever.

That drought was a harsh teacher. I learned, above all else, that it took time and patience to conserve. It was easy to let the tap run, leave the light burning, or the television on standby. It took effort and wit to collect the washing machine water, or catch the shower run off in a bucket for handwashing clothes. While I shunned the effort, those tasks brought me into a direct and immediate relationship with the hearth, the hub of human survival. Domestic habits were always about the fulfillment of basic needs – food, water and shelter. The modern, appliance-laden, electricity dependent, gloriously labour-saving kitchen took away the spirit from the hearth, replacing it with dings, beeps and electrical whirrs. I would never have happily foregone refrigeration, but as for the rest, I knew it could be replaced with muscle and ingenuity. The only trouble was, I did not want to be the one saddled with the labour.

By late November I decided I was suffering from a new mental health disorder. I called it LOWS, or Lack-of-Water Stress. I'd become tense. After suffering another bout of back pain from the washing up, twinges in my buttock from carrying twenty-litre buckets uphill, and managing to tangle the hose while watering the terraces – a task for the saintly patient due to the unpressurised water flow – I stormed towards the annex and kicked a plastic bucket, smashing it to pieces in frustration. Sitting on the pew outside the annex, trying to restore my equanimity, I was suddenly flooded with homesickness – for a place where it rained, like Ghana. In that moment I felt a tremendous solidarity with the women of Pampawie who faced a far more challenging domestic routine every day, not least, collecting water from the village pump.

But before long, my musings took me back to England and my old house on Boot Hill where it was forever green, and Jo next door, dear voluptuous Jo, who'd urged me to come here, who'd given me her blessing and drove me to the airport to say goodbye. I would never forget her embrace that day, how we'd stood in the middle of the airport lounge hugging and sobbing. We parted only to hold each other again, several more times before we could draw ourselves apart. We both knew it was permanent; I knew she would never write. Last I heard she'd moved. I had no idea where to.

I fought back the tears and scowled at the drought's bitter dry thrusting this life in my face with a mocking wind, sick of seeing a parched landscape of sandy yellows and browns, and green plastic tree guards.

Taking a break from the blazing sun, Greg joined me under the annex roof.

'No wonder Australians have coined the term 'battler', I murmured, feigning a smile.

He took in the shards of plastic that were once a bucket

scattered across the crazy paving without comment. Instead he said, 'Someone prepared to do battle. It is the land of the battler. Just think of the harsh lives of those early settlers, the pioneers. In the heat and the sun, building and farming.'

They were words of reassurance but inwardly, I shooed them away like bush flies.

'I don't know how you do it,' I said bitterly. 'How can you stand it out there in full sun?'

'I'm all right. You know me. I have to do it. I don't have a choice.'

'You do. No one has to work that hard.'

'Isobel, we are all desperately keen to have a house. Besides, I enjoy the challenge. It's like life drawing. Artists ask how I can hold a difficult pose for up to an hour, and it's the same thing; it's the challenge.'

'Well I don't feel the same. I hate the dry. Somehow, I never imagined Voltaire's Garden like this. I guess I've been caught in a European fantasy. Where things are lush, the grass green, the sap rising, all babbling brooks and cool mountain breezes. Where is all the new life?'

'Come on, we *have* given birth to a house and a garden in only six months. Don't give yourself a hard time.'

'But Voltaire's Garden is gasping. It's all right for you. The dry is ideal for building.'

He reached over and planted a kiss on my forehead before heading back to the building site. I stayed where I was, my gaze fixed on the bits of bucket.

The drought continued to suck at my spirit until I was bereft of all happy, uplifting thoughts and feelings, until I felt angry at the notion that this situation I was in could ever atone for the disastrous choice I made in leaving England. How could any of this 'be for the best'. What possible argument could the Pangloss's of the world envisage that could justify an optimistic interpretation of drought? Drought caused by human-created climate change, too. Had to be, despite what the gainsayers claimed. The consequences of which were so dire, not just for me, but for the whole of humanity and the planet. What argument could the Optimists put to that other than one that equated goodness with death, believed it was our fate to suffer, and that it was God's will flowing through humanity that had allowed wanton pollution, land degradation and the over-use of natural resources, all in the name of avarice and power, combined with an unrestrained copulation induced human plague. It was a human lack of moral responsibility and restraint that had led us into this mess, not God's will. If this was how our world was meant to be, and this was the best of all possible worlds, then for heaven's sake, what would the others have looked like?

CHAPTER FOUR

ONE MAN, ONE HAMMER, ONE HOUSE

'He was all brilliance. He gave me continued flashes of wit...
He had bold flights. He had humour. He had an
extravagance; he had a forcible oddity of style...He hummed
a ballad; he repeated nonsense.'

JAMES BOSWELL, IN *VOLTAIRE IN EXILE*

It was early December and the temperature was predicted
to reach thirty-five degrees. Another hot and dry day. In the
shade of the laundry, I watched Greg struggle up a ladder
balancing a six-metre length of timber in one arm. I looked
away, preferring not to see him heave the timber onto the
bedroom wall frame, some four metres off the ground. When I
looked again, the timber was in place, another mammoth effort
in a long succession of mammoth building tasks. I dashed to the
garden tap and filled the buckets, the sun already hot on my
back. I was more relaxed and less despondent now that Greg

was preparing the frames for the roof trusses, and soon we would have a roof.

As I returned to the annex with two sloshing buckets, a large, shiny, orange and black wasp cruised past me heading for the caravans. Looked like hornet. My skin prickled and my heart started pounding in my chest. I dumped the buckets and ran for the annex door.

Once inside I turned and peered through the window, glimpsing again the evil-looking insect. It was about three centimetres long, with orange wings and legs and an orange band around its abdomen. Even looking through the window I didn't feel safe, my panic certain it had to be aggressive being that size, with the worst sting imaginable, one no doubt likely to cause a severe allergic reaction and possible death.

I kept a wary eye on the beast. Before long, the wasp disappeared. When it returned it had a large huntsman spider three times its size in its mandibles, and it was dragging the spider along the crazy paving. Curiosity cooled my fear. I grew fascinated as the wasp inched backwards, struggling to drag the spider across the paving. Its determination was impressive.

Knowing almost nothing about wasps, I jumped on the Internet and typed 'spider eating wasp' into the search engine. The first Australian sites included the phrase 'spider wasp', a photograph in one of them confirming its identity. I discovered that mean-looking beast was solitary and docile. Its appearance aimed to shock and it certainly worked. The wasp liked hot, dry weather, and preferred to live in clay and sand piles. Our building site was the ideal habitat.

I returned to the window as Greg approached the laundry to fill his water bottle. The wasp dropped its prey and flew off. Moments later, Greg walked away. The coast clear again, the wasp returned and continued to drag the spider away.

I was relieved. I didn't want fear to dominate my thoughts,

to inhabit and inhibit my life. Yesterday, when I was washing up, I heard someone approach me from behind. I knew, rationally, that it was Greg, but when he called out my name my body jolted and I heard myself yelp. I wouldn't have been worried but I'd also developed a ludicrous fear of driving. For two decades I'd avoided night trips, since the night I drove into a volcanic dry-stone wall. I couldn't recall the accident – I lost consciousness before impact. A few minutes later I awoke with the car upside-down, motor running and petrol dripping on my head, convinced I was about to be burnt alive. I wasn't; I escaped unharmed, but severely shaken. Now, for a reason I couldn't fathom, I'd become fearful and resistant of driving full stop, not only at night, but at any time of day. Maybe I was carrying too much stress. Perhaps the pressure of the build was having a negative impact on my inner life. I needed to relax, take time out, go for a coffee or a swim. Instead, I mirrored Greg and worked from dawn till dusk seven days a week.

The summer dragged on. Alone in the annex on hot days, I knew there was nothing for it but to ride out the fierce sun, the wind, the dry. I also knew Greg would work all day. I was just as keen, but my body refused to cooperate. Whenever he walked in for a break, I could see he was suffering too, from continual exposure and relentless hard work. The drought meant he had not taken a single day of rest from the building since September. Slumped in a chair he looked exhausted; his eyes no longer sparkled, his head drooped, and his muscle-bound shoulders were knotted.

Now the frames were up and he was preparing them for the roof trusses, it was a tense time for him. He didn't have any phobias like me but he disliked heights, and balancing a six-metre length of hardwood as he carried it up a flimsy ladder was not easy. He needed help. But he was staunchly independent, preferring to work alone rather than ask a mate. I dare not even mention Bryan next door. Greg would have dismissed my suggestion in an instant. It was as if his masculinity was at stake, his pride. My role so far had involved holding the dummy-end of a tape measure, setting up and packing away tools, helping with the water level when we needed to check heights, stacking and re-stacking the timber, and assisting in raising the wall frames.

When it came to the trusses, things would be different. After plenty of advice and helpful tips about how to swing them into position, Greg realised doing it alone was too much to contemplate. He knew I'd be of little use, my fear of heights far surpassed my wasp phobia, or my fear of driving.

We always seemed lucky when it came to enlisting help in Cobargo. Our excavator John proved an excellent asset, and in many respects the form of our garden was the result of his shrewd decisions. Charlie was simply terrific of course, and now we had the pleasure of employing our friend Gino, a builder we met two years ago when he and his wife Patto came to collect their daughter and Mary's friend Polly from our house. They, too, were enthusiastic gardeners who shared our love of fresh food, cultivating what they could of their four hundred acres of bush near the head of the Brogo Dam.

Gino arrived in his old Holden ute the following morning. His burly frame, housed in baggy blue workpants and T-shirt, inspired confidence, but with his unkempt hair and bushy beard he looked wild and in a moment of fancy I thought he could pass for the Yaroma, the primeval beast said to live in the Brogo Wilderness. Like Big Foot or the Yeti, rumoured sightings and footprints were the only confirmation of the Yaroma's existence.

Many one of the men who lived on the fringes of the wilderness around here might have been mistaken for the Yaroma – like Gino, they all seemed to have a wild look about them. There must be an entire demographic of disenfranchised males in the area seeking a way of life far from the judgmental eyes of mainstream society, where their practical skills and ingenuity could find expression, or where they could carouse in Dionysian style tucked away in the gum trees. They owner-built in straw, mud brick and stone, and stood around braziers at parties drinking beer and bemoaning the sorry state of the urban world. These men were not tree-changers, they were fringe dwellers, men and women who had dropped-out of the rat race when their contemporaries forged careers in the city. And I warmed to some of them and I loved their wild side, pleased they'd found somewhere to belong, a haven, knowing it wasn't fair or right that modern society should lack spaces for individuals who don't fit the cardboard-cut-out consumer model of a man.

It was the first time Gino had seen our new place and, like everyone else, he was impressed with the views. As I approached, he was staring into the distance, stroking his beard. Standing beside him, his soft brown eyes and gentle, refined voice dissolved the impression his stature conjured. He was a giant, yes, but a cultured one.

'Great spot you've got up here.'

Everyone said the same.

He pointed into the distance to the south. 'That's where we are, over there, behind the mountain.'

I looked past Cobargo and down the valley, where the hills rose to meld with Murrabrine Mountain. I remembered Charlie pointing in the same direction.

'That's where our timber comes from.'

'So, you're the reason for all the noise out the back of our place. We can hear a spot mill. I wondered who was out there.'

'We must come out there ourselves sometime. If we ever get the time that is. We never go anywhere at the moment.'

'You're building. It goes like that. Let's look at the trusses. Did they give you any plans?'

I led Gino over to where the trusses were lying on the ground and then headed off to fetch the plans. Greg was climbing down a ladder at the rear of the build as I passed.

After some time and discussion as to which truss went where, Gino took charge. I stood by in a small patch of shade as together the men raised the trusses upside-down onto the frames one by one. Then they flipped the trusses upright and nailed them into position. Gino made it look effortless.

Once several trusses were in place, Gino insisted we braced them. By then, I couldn't stand around craning my neck any longer and headed back to the caravans. From my vantage at the annex window, I watched, amazed, as he took a length of bracing steel, climbed up the wall frames like a monkey and walked along the trusses as if he were on the ground. He might not have had the stature of a ballet dancer, but he had the same balance and grace. Holding the bracing as a balancing pole, he might as well have been pirouetting across the trusses, he looked so confident. I couldn't help myself and nicknamed him the Ballerina.

The two days it took to erect and brace the trusses were a welcome reprieve for Greg. Like a prisoner released from solitary confinement, an only child finding a playmate; his spider-waspish, single-handed, single-minded determination was restrained enough in Gino's presence to allow the other Greg expression – the gregarious Greg, perky, witty and entertaining.

As Gino packed up his gear, we stood by his ute facing our soon-to-be home, now almost twenty metres of wall frames supporting roof trusses crisscrossed with steel strap. There was a good deal of steel strap wrapped around the subfloor too, and bracing the walls. Our property was in a high wind area, a grade down from cyclonic, and that strap would stop the house from collapsing in a wind blast. The bracing was compulsory, a government requirement meant for lightweight pine wall studs. Our frames were hardwood but we needed the bracing just the same.

An observation by me that our house had more metal in it than timber and Greg sparked up with his favourite diatribe on the modern world of useless tools and materials designed for maximum profit and minimum integrity. Greg loved to rant, he was never happier than when his Slovenian blood was pumping, his dander up over yet another ineffectual product from the hardware store.

Gino laughed and waved us goodbye. I watched his ute head off along the driveway and disappear down Blackbutt Drive with a touch of sadness. We really needed the company.

It was the weekend again and Greg turned back into his solitary self. He was up at four, pottering around in the garden. He came back inside to wolf down a bowl of cereal and then he was out in the heat climbing the trusses to nail battens for the roofing iron. Kettle in hand, I held my breath as he struggled with another batten, heaving it up to the roof. As he lined the batten in position, movement on the paving diverted my attention. The spider wasp was back, only this time it was not alone. It seemed to be engaged in a violent looking struggle with another spider wasp. I stepped back from the window as Sarah approached from behind.

'Get the camera,' I said.

'What is it?'

I pointed at the wasps writhing on the paving.

Sarah raced into the office caravan and returned with our chunky digital camera. She went outside, brave enough to step close. I stayed indoors.

'What are they doing?' Sarah asked when she came back in, scrolling through her shots.

'I thought at first they were fighting but now I think they might be mating.'

'It looks violent.'

'We should leave them be. Come on.'

She sat on the sofa with *Dolly* magazine. I braced myself for the litany of 'I wants' that was sure to follow. Mary was on the Internet and Pickles, who'd taken no interest in the wasps, dozed on the pew outside. None of them needed anything from me. They only wanted feeding as and when they grew hungry and that was about it. Fifteen-year-olds amounted to having aliens in the house, so far removed were they from being children or adults or anything resembling human. Their moods ranged from sullen indifference to smouldering anger and they majored in being adversarial. In the face of their teenage attitude, I was grateful they never reneged on their watering schedule.

It was mid-morning when I took my harvesting basket and headed down to the terraces. There were three of them now, flattened save for a few humps of topsoil at the far ends. Three long curves of earth with embankments a metre high, following the contours of the hillside. Later we would create paths below the embankments on the second and third terraces, with a series of short paths extending at right angles towards the terrace edge. The remaining soil would be retained with lengths of re-used corrugated iron – currently stacked on the granite outcrop on the high side behind the house – to make raised beds. In the meantime, I'd improvised by making mulch borders to contain the vegetables in grave-like garden beds.

I'd planted capsicums, cucumbers, beans, basil, zucchinis, carrots, potatoes and, filling most of the third terrace, tomatoes. I could water the whole area with the hose. To conserve water and protect the vegetables from the harsh summer sun and wind, the beds were heavily mulched with paddock clippings about a foot thick, relying on the wool bale and heaps of rotting clippings over by the head of our dam. Drought meant no mowing. Although we had purchased another lawn mower after Greg killed the first through overuse. No one could understand why we didn't buy a ride-on but Greg had slipped a disk in his lower back and complained ride-on mowers gave him back pain. I couldn't understand the logic in his argument since I was the one saddled with all the mowing now Greg was building, but I didn't argue. There were some things you just couldn't argue about with Greg.

The season was still early and there was little to harvest. I picked a couple of ripening tomatoes and a few beans.

I was listless. Our plumber Acko was coming on Monday to put the roof on the house. I was desperate to have a roof to provide some shade; the red and apple gums on the granite outcrop and the stand of red gums in the gully beside the dam were too far from the house site to provide any. Until the trees I planted six months earlier gained height, the roof of the house would provide the only shelter from the sun. It was not easy for me to apply what scant patience I had to this, knowing how long I would need to wait for trees to grow canopies. I could already see that Voltaire's Garden was going to test that impatient spirit in me.

The weekend ticked by and when Acko arrived in his white ute, full of his usual *joie de vivre*, mobile phone in one hand and nail belt in the other, my belly filled with anticipation and I rushed outside. Greg was up on the roof nailing battens. In my capacity as project manager, I gave him crushing deadlines, poor guy.

'Are we all set?' Acko asked looking around, and I pointed to the corrugated iron sheets of deep, rich red, lying in stacks of various lengths between the driveway and the house. Beside them were lengths of gutter, flashing and fascia. Boxes of screws and fittings sat on a pile of timber on the sub-floor. Everything was ready.

'I'm third labourer, today,' I joked. 'I want to help.'

'Good. There'll be plenty to do.'

'Only, I'm staying at ground level.' Three rungs up a ladder was my limit.

Acko laughed. 'Have I missed coffee?'

'I'll put the kettle on.'

We headed to the annex.

Ever since Acko replaced the roof on Greg's cottage, we'd been been friends, the kind that rarely see each other but feel the warmth when they do. Maybe our conviviality originated the day I gave Acko a large jar of my homemade jalapeno-chili sauce. Every time I saw him after that he told me he was still eating it, and that it was so fiery, he only needed to use the coating of a spoon to spice his dinner.

Greg joined us in the annex and took up a chair.

'I see you've been busy, Greg.'

I lowered my gaze. He was always busy, but more since last week, as I'd organized Acko to start on the roof without realising the need for roofing battens to screw the iron to.

'I'll start on the fascia and guttering so you can carry on battening.' He turned to me. 'You won't see any iron on the roof today. Sorry to disappoint.' His eyes twinkled as he smiled. He knew how keen I was to have a roof.

All day I stood around at the bottom of Acko's ladder like a little girl watching her father make a doll's house, eager and expectant, wanting to help at every moment, not prepared to leave just in case I missed an opportunity. Acko humoured me, letting me hand him tools, brackets and screws. I felt involved, even though at the end of the day he told me I'd probably saved him ten minutes.

Acko stopped work at four, leaving us another four hours of daylight. Greg used the time to add more battens to the roof until I called him in for dinner at sunset.

It was a grim evening meal. Even Mary and Sarah, aware of the tension emanating from a worn out and pressured Greg, were subdued.

The following day Acko arrived at seven. The forecast was a warm twenty-five degrees with an afternoon sea breeze. One of those perfect days, the one's that draw people to this area, which is said to have more of those perfect days in a year than most places.

'Ready for a big day?' he said to me.

'Yep.'

Greg had been on the roof for the last hour nailing the last of the battens. I felt terrible causing him to work so hard but another part of me was indifferent. Greg was a workaholic. It was how he burned up all his fiery energy. Hard work kept him happy, kept him strong and lean and how he liked to be. Hard work was an integral part of his identity. Greg didn't do boredom. He was one of those men who would stretch a task to make it last just so he could keep busy. And I was certainly not interested in his mood.

He was sullen at breakfast and I hadn't had the courage to talk to him since. I found it wiser to avoid grumpy, agitated or otherwise stressed men on building sites, and I was greatly relieved when he called out to Acko as we passed on our way to the roofing iron, and we both looked up to see his smiling face emerging from a confusion of roof timber.

'I'll be right down.'

'No rush. Isobel can help me set up.'

Leaving Greg to finish the battens, we walked around the house to where we were working yesterday.

'The first sheets to go up are the short ones,' Acko said. 'Before we put any up, can you cut lengths of sisalation?'

'Sure.'

At last, something useful to do. I found scissors, a tape measure and a ruler. Sisalation came with its own kind of awkwardness – unwieldy, uncooperative and slippery – and I was reminded of the geo-textile matting I rolled out on septic day. I cut lengths to pass to Acko now on the roof, and unstacked the smaller sheets of iron, carrying them to where needed. Best of all, I got to weather the iron with a shifter, bending one end of the corrugations forward to create lips that would prevent rainwater from travelling up the iron and into the roof space.

At ground level, I had it easy. Greg, who had at last stopped battening, climbed a ladder holding an iron sheet, passed it to Acko, then climbed further to align its bottom edge. Acko, on the roof, screwed the sheet in place. It was a process repeated over and again, sheet after sheet, Acko in cap, sunglasses, shorts and volleys, walking on the roof with his drill and screws, confident, self-assured, his powerful thighs countering the thirty-degree pitch. Greg, poor thing, was up and down, and up and down ladders, back and forth with my sisalation cut to size and then my weathered iron sheets. His job was to peer along gutters to check the alignment. He tired quickly. The sheets became as light as a kite when carried by the breeze, and as heavy as lead when Greg tried to steer the sheets in alternative directions to the wind. Corrugated iron in a wind could decapitate like a guillotine; I watched ready to help.

Acko, meanwhile, was so happy on the roof he burst into song. He had a gig on Friday in his band Fig Jam. He used our roof as a stage, entertaining us with old classics like Don

McClean's 'American Pie', and endless songs by The Small Faces and The Kinks. Spurred by Acko's bonhomie, Greg remembered snatches of songs, then Acko amazed us both by singing every verse and chorus.

He was with us for two weeks. Every day I heard him on the roof, humming, whistling or singing, roused by Greg's repertoire of song snatches.

When he left on the last day, I no longer stared into a shade-less building site from the annex window. It was such a relief I almost forgot it was Christmas. The house provided the only festive feel around us, with its new red roof sheltering our jailhouse of timber studs.

Mary and Sarah were now on school holidays, spending their days hanging around the annex, or walking back and forth from their caravan. The last seven months had not been easy for them. Mary had recently moved schools to further her burgeoning musical talent, while Sarah's childish petulance had grown into contemptuous defiance. For teenagers, I knew they were good, bright kids, but they still caused their mother much anguish and distress.

I wanted to create a nice Christmas for them, but none of us were in the festive spirit, especially not Greg. His focus was solely on the house, and now we had a roof he had more work to do, not to meet a deadline I'd created, but one the weather had.

Since the onset of the drought, I'd viewed the weather forecasts on the Internet. On Christmas Eve, I found rain predicted after Boxing Day. That meant water in the tank if Greg could connect the down pipes in time.

Waking up to Christmas in a caravan on a building site felt bizarre, a few cards scattered on shelves the only festive feel in the annex, and I was heavy-hearted when I thought of the girls and the lack of a proper Christmas. I recalled the deluge of cards I received as a teacher, the way I'd tacked them to the white board, leaving an ever-shrinking space in the centre, one that encouraged an even greater flood of cards.

My parents were spending the day with my sister, Michele, and her family. We were not invited. Things had been awkward between us since I met Greg, choosing to be with a man they did not believe right for me. And that was mostly due to the way he behaved around them, witty yet acerbic and wilfully controversial. He liked to antagonise. There was nothing I could do to stop him. Or that antagonism would have fallen on me.

Since I'd been with Greg, I'd become more and more isolated from my family and, idiosyncratically, almost everybody else it seemed. I'd been slow to make friends here, my normally gregarious self, alienated and lonely. My growing sense of belonging to the land had not been matched by the same sense of belonging to its people. I could scarcely believe five years had passed and I still felt so much pain over the loss of the Ghana Link, my old home in Boot Hill, and my friends, especially Jo, who invited me to share Christmas Day with her the year my mother returned to Australia. It wasn't like me to hold on so tightly to the past and for so long. What on earth was the matter with me?

I had hoped Voltaire's Garden would be my salvation. It had the potential – a perfect place for creativity, so peaceful and lovely – but I wondered if it would be enough. Toiling in the garden was satisfying, but we were so isolated, two solitary workers on a hill. Hermits. Greg praised me continuously, admiring my determination, but I had limits, I couldn't use power tools or build granite dry-stone walls. Often, I felt he would have fared better with a robust woman with skills to match his own. Had I made yet another calamitous mistake, by failing to take account of one not insignificant detail in the project – the workload?

Noticing the girls' caravan door open, I rallied myself, deciding to make an effort, if not for me, then for them. Greg's parents had invited us for Christmas lunch. The day was already bright, the sky a clear blue. I looked at our new red roof, smart and proud like Santa's hat, and forced a smile. At least our house had the right feel to it.

After breakfast, Greg took a break from building to water the terraces while I prepared lunch. Cooking in the annex always posed a challenge, it was awkward and cramped, my day-to-day cooking revolving around simplicity and the dirtying of as little as possible. I was sure I'd feel a whole lot better when I had my own kitchen, one with a pantry, a sink, bench space and room to swing. Today, however, I decided to make an effort. Voltaire's Garden had begun to produce a good summer harvest and I planned to incorporate as much fresh produce as possible into the Christmas lunch. Loving kindness expressed with food was my way of making others, and myself, feel better. After all fresh food, well-prepared, inspired celebration and goodwill.

Instead of roasting meats in the heat of summer, I'd simmered a chicken last night. I would have roasted it but our oven was so slow it only cooked fruit cake. After de-boning and dicing the meat, I rushed out to the herb terrace for a bunch of French tarragon to use in a garlic and tarragon mayonnaise. To accompany that, I made a potato salad using our very first potatoes, dressed with capers, and fresh mint, tarragon and garlic chives all from the garden. A large bunch of carrots made a sweet carrot and sultana salad, and our bush beans became French bean vinaigrette.

Embracing the festive mood, I wore the shocking pink dress Greg purchased for a few dollars in a charity shop in Narooma some months before. It was made by a well-known Australian fashion designer and local resident Pru Acton, and wearing it felt like being an eastern European in costume. Following my lead, Greg donned a romantic calico shirt and jeans. He looked dashing no matter what he wore and today he was my knight without armour. Sarah decided on a bright green dress with white polka dots and Mary wore her usual black T-shirt and jeans, her never brushed long red hair hanging over her face like a poorly-drawn curtain. Together we looked like stand-ins for an *Adam's Family* shoot. Perfect!

It was a pleasant drive north to Narooma, a charming fishing, tourist and retirement town hugging a vast lagoon, and Carolyn and Jack were in good spirits when we arrived, greeting us with their usual bonhomie. Jack had some fine wine ready to pour, and sounds of old-school jazz played in the background. I felt mellow the moment I walked in.

Jack's eyes lit up when he saw the food.

'Is this all from the garden?'

'Everything but the chicken.'

'Ah,' he smiled and I glowed in his appreciation.

After quaffing wine and gorging on the food, by the end of lunch my eyes were more than a little glazed. We sat around the table and let Greg and Carolyn entertain us with reminiscences of their days in Singapore and Washington. Before long, out came the family photos.

Carolyn and Jack had adopted Greg at birth. Carolyn was raised in Tupelo, Mississippi, in the upper echelons of Southern society. She met Jack, a poor Victorian dairy farmer's son, in Japan during the occupation after the Second World War. She was a secretary in the Office of Strategic Services, and he a debonair young Australian Army officer. Following their wedding, Jack returned to Melbourne with his new bride. After weathering the frustrations of childlessness, they took the advice of a neighbour, then manageress of a foundling home, and decided to adopt. A short time later a sickly asthmatic baby covered in infantile eczema arrived at the home. Introductions were duly arranged, Carolyn fell in love, and baby Greg was soon in her care. She put him on goat's milk and saved his life.

Greg spent his childhood moving from posting to posting, living overseas in Singapore and the United States, and around Australia. He, along with his adopted sister, grew up surrounded by the dwindling privileges of Australia's officer class, the champagne, parties and endless cocktail parties of military high society in the 1960s, especially when the family was posted to Washington DC where Jack served as military attaché. Poor Greg had to avoid excitement for fear of asthma. Luckily, he was a serious young fellow, as living, for him, was a serious enterprise.

His life was also full of adventure. In 1958, when Jack and Carolyn returned to Australia from Jack's posting in Singapore, Jack flew to Darwin in a military plane, leaving Carolyn and Greg, at the tender age of three, to make the journey on a Norwegian freighter, the 'Thörstrand', journeying along with the family car, a 1956 Zephyr. It was the freighter's final voyage before going to the scrap yard, chartered by a Norwegian professor for the collection and study of barnacles. The freighter was so old that the generators caught fire halfway through the erratic journey, somewhere between Borneo and Jakarta. Fortunately, the fire was extinguished without casualty.

For Greg, the drama didn't end there. After perplexing his mother with a most foul smell in their cabin, the result of his collection of barnacle specimens given to him by the professor in matchboxes which he stored under his bunk, he then proceeded to give poor Carolyn the fright of her life. The Captain had decided to provide the few child passengers with some entertainment by rigging up a swimming pool using a large crate strapped to the deck and lined with a tarpaulin. As the freighter pitched and rolled the seawater in the crate pool sloshed from one side to the other in a great wave. The children decided a game of chicken would be fun, involving diving under the water as it came surging towards them from the other side. Greg won the game, waiting until the very last moment before ducking under the wave. Only he was too late. The wave washed him out of the crate, hurling him through the air in a torrent of water towards the deck. He bounced twice and skittered towards the deck's edge, saved from falling overboard into the shark-infested waters below when his torso miraculously hit a stanchion. The sum total of his injuries was a grazed elbow and knee.

It was a story Carolyn loved to tell, and it was the first time providence had intervened to save his life. Like a cat with nine lives, he had survived one near electrocution, two lightning strikes, one backwards fall over a cliff and two head-on collisions in his car. None of these events seemed to have scarred him either. When I recalled how shaken I was after driving into a volcanic dry-stone wall one night in the Canary Islands, I was amazed at his indifference. I was still too scared to drive at night.

Too quickly it was three o'clock and time to leave.

On the way home, snaking our way through the towering forests that blanket the coastal plain around Gulaga – Mount Dromedary as it is also known – it occurred to me that this was the only day we'd taken off since moving up to the land in May, and we'd really needed it.

We returned early so Greg could finish connecting the last down pipes to the gutters. All that remained was the burying of a ten-metre stretch of pipe from the house to the tank.

Boxing Day we awoke to a fine mizzle. Greg ate a hurried

breakfast and went outside. The next time I saw him he was wearing his Driza-Bone – a large oilskin coat traditionally worn by Australian farmers on horseback to keep out the cold and wet weather – along with a wide brimmed oilskin hat. I watched from the annex as he hacked at the baked-solid ground with a mattock. The mizzle combined with clouds of dust billowing out of the trench, settling on him like confetti. Tucked inside his Driza-Bone on a warm, wet summer's day, he worked up a steamy sweat. With each blow of the mattock, he looked more like a mud-monster, clay confetti combining with sweat becoming rivulets of mud running down his cheeks. I made him take coffee and lunch breaks outside.

'The rain must be making it easier, surely,' I called through the window as he headed back for another go at the trench.

'It isn't, Isobel.' He was cryptic.

'But you're soaked!'

'The ground isn't. Believe me.'

Curious, I had to see for myself. Sheltering under an umbrella, I followed him to the trench. The mizzle seemed to float rather than fall, coating bone-dry surfaces everywhere but doing little else. The wettest soil around was clinging to Greg.

'You must be magnetic.'

'What?'

Building seemed to turn everyone deaf. I raised my voice.

'I'll leave you to it.'

I could see he was becoming irascible so I returned to the annex.

The mizzle that fell all that day and the next was far from enough to break the drought. We still adhered to our watering program using the one garden tap, buckets and watering cans, and the grass we hadn't mown for months was crisp underfoot. Fortunately, the mizzle had put water in the tank, removing some of the anxiety over our fresh water supply.

The following five days were dry again, and now it was New Year's Eve. Greg was puzzling over the best way to insert windows into the frames. He'd left the trench open in case of a leak at one of the joins. The powdery subsoil and lumpy clay piles dotted along the trench made it hard to get to the garden tap with a wheelbarrow, so with Greg's approval I took a shovel and began to backfill it.

Soon I heard voices. It was our neighbours, John and Hillary. They'd built their home on the same subdivision two years earlier, and now John was landscaping. When we moved up here we'd rarely seen them, but once they saw the roof they began to take an interest in our progress. From then on, from time to time they would drop by on a neighbourly pretext and their cheery smiles were a welcome treat.

'We're not interrupting, I hope,' Hillary said, her exuberant English accent generating that warm glow of cultural recognition inside my own English skin as she turned the corner of the annex. She was a trim, dark-haired woman with a kind, open face.

'Not at all,' I said, 'I'll show you around.'

Hillary had a joyous spirit and a cheery English laugh. She reminded me of my great-aunt Betty, my paternal grandfather's sister. We grew close in those years I spent in England when she became another mother to me and a fabulous grandmother for Mary and Sarah. Whenever I saw Hillary, I remembered Betty; they even looked the same. Quintessentially English in appearance and demeanour, they could both have had parts in an Agatha Christie whodunit.

John was more formal and serious. He was tall and slim with a shock of grey hair and he manifested the same persevering, practical qualities as Greg, but with an endearing English ethnicity. They'd come to Australia as South African expatriates, John retaining his passion for proteas.

'We stopped by to ask if Mary or Sarah would mind watering our garden while we're away,' John said as they surveyed our progress. By then we were down by the courtyard formed by the U of the house, where John and Hillary took in our back garden.

'We'll pay them, of course,' Hilary added.

'I'm sure one of them will do it. Mary probably.'

We cornered the end of the building and found Greg working on the west wing.

'Careful,' I said. 'Don't trip over the sewer pipe. It'll be buried under concrete eventually. Right now, it isn't very secure.'

Hillary's eyes were everywhere.

'This is looking tremendous. I expect you can't wait to see walls now that the roof is on. My word it's enormous.'

'It does seem large.'

'It *is* large.'

'It feels like a palace compared with the annex.'

Greg took a break and joined us. While he chatted to John, Hillary continued to express her admiration.

'Isobel, you must be exhausted, well both of you, of course. All this hard work.'

'It is a bit ridiculous, the scale of it.'

'We won't hold you up. I'm sure you've lots to do and it might rain,' she said, looking to the western sky where clouds were gathering over the mountains.

'I hope so. Before you leave, I must ask, do you like basil by any chance?'

Basil was my favourite herb, and I tended to grow a copious quantity each year to ensure I had plenty. That season the seed had germinated well and now I had two garden beds full of basil on the terraces. Continual tip pruning had stimulated prolific growth and prevented the plants from going to seed. It was my first bounteous crop on the land and I succumbed to a compulsion to give.

'But what would I do with it?' She looked bemused.

'We make pesto.'

'How do you make that?'

I talked her through the recipe.

'It's dead easy to make.'

'Then, yes, I will take some. I think I have pine nuts in the pantry. It sounds delightful.'

As John and Hillary left, the sun dipped behind a cloud. I spied Sarah heading for the annex and I could hear Mary in their caravan playing piano, back on her dark, menacing chords.

Greg went back to work and I ignored the trench and wandered around in the garden. It was pleasing to see the twelve fruit trees in the orchard terrace putting on some moderate growth in spite of the dry, and the olives in the rips below them looked healthy. It was even more gratifying to see the beginnings of green grass spreading across the transpiration bed, the result of my industrious mowing of soil, weeds and the occasional grass runner. Below, the row of citrus trees and native shrubs had developed new shoots. Beyond, gently rolling hills smattered with eucalypts met the mountains to the west, a perfect background completing an idyllic pastoral scene, beautiful despite the drought. The clouds thickened over the mountains, and I hoped the forecast would be accurate.

By eleven, the sky had darkened considerably. Alone in the annex, standing by the window while I prepared lunch, I heard a rush of air sweeping past, the rustle of leaves and the clatter of a toppled bucket. In moments large spots appeared on the paving. A thunderous boom made the ground shudder, then a dramatic fork of lightning struck the mountains.

Soon rain, glorious, glorious rain pounded the roof,

obliterating Mary's dark, death metal chords that could be heard even inside the annex, and I couldn't see the house just metres away. I wondered how the girls were coping stuck in their caravan. Before long a very wet Greg entered to find me dry, cosy and pleased. We watched as the windows misted, thrilled, relieved and anxious all at once, as the rain was so heavy, it had no time to drain away from the crazy paving, making its way under the annex door. In seconds, a small flood covered a third of our tiny living space. Greg moved the rug under the dining table. Keen not to let the water travel further, I rolled my pants up to my knees and swept the water out the door with a broom.

'It's like a beatification after years in purgatory,' I yelled above the din.

Greg was less enthusiastic. He was concerned for the building and once the heaviest rain had passed he went out to check on the site.

He returned relieved.

The rain stopped an hour later, and then he checked the tank. It was several centimetres fuller, and thankfully for the girls, there was respite from watering the garden.

New Year's Day felt the same for us as Christmas. It was as if living in the caravans had suspended large chunks of our life, locked us all into a compulsive race to the finish, as if only in a proper house could we all function normally. In many respects it was true. A contemporary western lifestyle relies heavily on having plenty of room and rooms – a place to sleep, a place to cook, another to eat, somewhere to lounge about and somewhere to study, all separate places for individual needs. Greg was less affected as he worked continuously outside, and I coped okay in the multifunctional annex when the girls were at school, but now they were home for the summer holidays and life in the annex was crowded and oppressive.

The manifest domestic tension put Greg in overdrive. He nailed all the external cladding to the wall studs – we were using cement sheeting – and fitted in place the thirty-two tall, narrow, windows I'd chosen with astounding speed, all in preparation for the next milestone – laying a floor. I helped too, escaping the annex to prime hundreds of metres of reveal and sill timber, which I straddled across the floor joists. Day by day and wall by wall the house became enclosed, until it was a shell bereft of ceiling and floor. It seemed to ache for clean lines and smooth finishes and rooms.

A long stack of Cyprus pine tongue-in-groove floorboards had been sitting under cover in the paddock for months. I'd bought them on special. At last, one sunny late-January day, we shunted half the floorboards into the house. They smelled so fresh and looked so new and smooth I could hardly wait to see them laid.

Greg felt the same way, only he wished he could screw up his eyes, make a wish and bingo, the floor was there before him, nailed, sanded and sealed. Instead, he straddled the floor joists in that cavernous space, one man, one chisel, and a hammer. I stood in a doorway as he rolled out roof blanket – insulation backed sisalation – over the joists for under-floor insulation, with the silver side down, the fibreglass insulation exposed. Then he selected a board. Kneeling on a plank laid across the insulation and joists, he slowly worked his way along, nailing the board off at sixty-centimetre intervals with a hammer. We couldn't use a staple gun for fear it would split the timber; Cyprus was too brittle and hardwood joists, too hard. He wanted to use floor cramps too, but he couldn't devise a way to use them.

Another two boards finished the first thirteen-metre length. The boards were seven centimetres wide. He had another eighteen metres to go.

'Don't look behind you,' I said.

'I know. I can't bear it.'

I wasn't surprised. I looked at all that space and the one solitary board nailed in place. It was barely visible.

Greg selected a board for the next row, positioned it, and then jammed it with his hands as tight as he could against its sister board, forcing it even tighter with hammer and chisel.

I had never known him so intent on getting a job done. He worked all day on his knees, cramping and nailing board after board. All day and well into the evening the girls and I sat listening to the sound of the hammer echoing through the building. Bang, bang, bang, meant a nail went in well, more bangs and Greg had reached a particularly hard joist, and any cries of pain meant he had hit his thumb.

Greg's wit and sense of humour had disappeared. Instead he developed an asperity of temper equal, no doubt, to the suffering his body endured, and in the two weeks it took him to lay the floor, he drove his already tired body beyond its limits. A baker's cyst on his left knee that had developed during the renovations of the cottage, now swelled to bursting proportions whenever he knelt or crawled around, causing him considerable discomfort and, through constant kneeling, we thought he'd torn some cartilage in his right knee. It was painfully swollen and immobile; he had difficulty putting on socks.

Yet he remained fixed and determined as ever. I admired his passion and resolve, but began to fret for his body. He refused to see a doctor, and I was sure his injuries were far worse than my wrenched gluteus maximus. With two sore knees, he hung the four exterior doors to secure the house from the rain – an easier job as he got to stand – leaving open a section of the north wall facing into our courtyard, where a ten-millimetre thick pane of glass, almost two and a half metres tall and just as wide would go. We'd got it cheap as part of an order cancelled by a shop. The glass was so heavy we needed help to fit it in place. Greg habitually screened the hole with a tarpaulin each night to protect the floor against dampness and the possibility, however remote, of more rain.

A week later it was February. We'd been on the dole a whole year. I despised claiming unemployment benefits. The humiliation gnawed at me, even as I knew it was a tradition among owner builders. We'd been living in the caravans for far too long, working like demons to get our new enterprise up and running, and we were a long way from any kind of self-sufficient, sustainable lifestyle, let alone opening a B&B. The only other income Greg had coming in was an occasional life-drawing gig and my wages from the Cobargo post office, a two-hour a week casual position I'd taken on last month thinking it would do me good. The work provided a change of scene and a chance to connect with the community.

That night we'd been invited to our first social engagement since Christmas and the first, independent of Greg's family, since we'd moved into the caravans last May. I was determined to make the night a turning point. I was tired of the isolation and I berated myself for not making the effort to establish relationships with the many wonderful women I'd met in Cobargo. I'd been grieving for too long the loss of old friends. Today, I had my heart set on enjoying myself and I already felt excited.

It was Laura's fiftieth birthday party. Like Patto and Gino, I'd come to know Laura and her husband Peter through their daughter Vanessa, another of Mary and Sarah's friends. Laura taught at the primary school in the heritage village of Tilba Tilba up the coast and Peter was an electrician. In spite of my affectionate feelings towards them, it was almost a year since I last visited their property in Coolagolite, a locality five kilometres from Cobargo heading towards the coast.

The party started at six. At eleven I drove into Cobargo to sort mail. I parked the car in the Cobargo Co-op's car park and as I crossed the road I took in at a glance all the shops and businesses owned and run by people I knew, one way or another. How much I loved this town with all of its rich history and quaint old buildings. The post office itself was a rendered brick building of late-nineteenth century construction, with thick walls and high ceilings and double-hung windows, an important building made to last.

The proprietor Peter greeted me at the counter and ushered me through to the back. He was a happy-go-lucky guy with a fancy beard and a glint in his eye, always ready to engage in light banter. He had a passion for motorbikes as did his wife Sylvia, and they were also keen gardeners and foodies.

The mail had arrived early, four boxes crammed with envelopes stacked on a swivel chair.

Rural addresses required local knowledge; some residents had mailboxes at the post office, many were post restante, the rest went out on one of four mail runs. Making the sort harder, some residents had several names, some had identical names and different addresses, and some addresses involved many different surnames. Separations and divorces could be tricky and the old farming families, the Tarlintons, Tyrrells and Salways had numerous locations for various family branches, in boxes, on the counter, or on the runs. Even after Sylvia's extensive training, things were not much clearer.

'It's like a crash course in a community who's who,' I said, after the tenth time I'd interrupted Peter to ask for help.

He laughed.

'They're on the counter. You still haven't worked that out yet. Coffee?'

'Please.'

Intent on meeting the one o'clock sorting deadline and to compensate for my deficiency in memory recall, I worked with dogged concentration.

When Peter returned, he strolled to the parcel desk, ambling to the counter whenever customer a entered the building.

'Do you like Zappa?'

'Frank? I do.'

I was impressed. I knew Peter and Sylvia were Harley riders, but Zappa too! Peter's casual, public service appearance belied great musical taste. We escaped into the soundtrack to *Baby Snakes* for the next hour.

Back on the building site, Greg worked despite his knees. He was preparing to erect the interior walls. He'd laid out a large green tarpaulin to protect the floor from his chaotic concatenation of tools and materials and was busy ferrying in timber. After a brief exchange, I left him and his mess and entered the annex.

I surveyed the room before taking in the bowl of sliced cucumbers I'd left soaking in brine on the kitchen cabinet. The spiced vinegar I'd made for the last batch of pickling would be enough for this batch too. I searched cupboards for suitable jars. Pickling cucumbers was easy, it was the one form of preserving I was prepared to tackle in the annex.

Outside, I watered the garden and harvested vegetables. Mary and Sarah arrived home at four thirty and my time was then absorbed in the blow by blow accounts of their respective day's dramas. It was almost six when I went down to the house and suggested to Greg he packed up as we were now late for the party.

'What about the tarpaulin?' I said as Greg made to ease himself down from the front door of the house.

'Don't bother. What chance is there of rain?'

I looked up doubtfully at the overcast sky.

'The rain never blows in from the north,' he said, full of confidence.

When we arrived at Laura and Peter's house, the party was well underway. Mary and Sarah headed straight towards the back of the house where their friends were gathered. I strolled beside Greg, who was limping and in considerable discomfort. While I had dressed demurely in brown and white, he wore a brightly-striped, red and orange jacket and tight black pants, odd attire for someone in a taciturn mood. He had not been jolly since his knee injuries.

Laura greeted us on the veranda. She was garbed in a dark-blue, strapless dress and looked sexy and gorgeous. Her appearance seemed out of character for a normally measured and reserved Laura, both in appearance and personality. I was stunned to see her looking so glamourous.

'Good to see you.' We exchanged a kiss.

'Lovely to be here.'

'Peter's inside. Help yourself to a drink.'

We found Peter in the kitchen pouring wine. He was as ebullient as ever, beaming from ear to ear, exuding his familiar Italian-Australian charm.

'You made it!'

'Sure did.'

'What can I get you? Beer? Wine? Here, meet my brother. You haven't met before? Excuse me, nearly spilled it.' He laughed. 'Food's behind you,' he added, pointing, before getting distracted by other guests.

A small and lively band played in the living room. The kitchen and dining rooms were crammed with guests, the crowd spilling outside onto a large, deep veranda. The atmosphere was exhilarating. How exalted I felt to be there. For a very brief moment I recalled my fortieth back in England, when fifty friends joined me for a night at a plate-smashing Greek restaurant, replete with sexy male dancers. But never mind that, I told myself, grabbing a glass.

Greg limped out to the veranda, finding somewhere quiet to sit, while I joined in conversations about food, gardening and the wonders of Italy, determined to enjoy every moment. The band played a number of sets, people danced, the birthday cake was cut, and by nine, the party created a wall of sound that muffled the rumblings from the sky above, making those inside unaware of the rain pounding the roof. I heard the rain and ignored it.

After months with no social life, I drank, ate and danced until midnight, ecstatic, my brown skirt swinging to the rhythms of classic 80s hits. After the band's last set, we listened to a party mix including my favourite band Talking Heads. I once had a crush on David Byrne, a crush that lasted for two decades. He, and the culture he represented, was a major factor in my leaving Cobargo for England in 1981. It was ironic to be here now, dancing to the same music in Laura's living room.

Several women of around my age joined me, swaying and rolling their hips, pointing their fingers in the air, while our teenaged daughters laughed hysterically in the hallway. Meanwhile Greg lingered on the veranda, idly chatting to men abandoned by their wives in favour of the music.

The rain eased a little on the drive home, but we could tell by the surface water and roadside puddles that it had been heavy. We arrived home at one. Greg headed straight for the building. He came back looking worried.

'The floor is flooded,' he said grimly.

I thought it *never* rains from the north. I didn't say it. Greg would have flipped if I had. 'What will we do?'

'Nothing until the morning.'

At dawn we entered the building. One fifth of the floor was water damaged. Nail heads were already rusting and boards were threatening to cup and bow. Before I could think of how to save the floor, Greg crawled under the house to slit the under-floor insulation he'd so painstakingly laid out only weeks before, to allow any water that had dripped down through the floorboards to drain out.

He returned, flustered. His eyes had narrowed to slits and he wore a moody frown.

'How the hell are we going to dry the floor?' he said.

The way he said it made me feel I was somehow to blame. Pardon me for having a good time.

'I've dried wet patches with a hairdryer in the past. It works quite well.'

He stopped in his tracks as though a light had gone on in his head and his demeanour softened.

'I'll get little beaver.'

He returned with a small electric blower, attached a long hose, and for the rest of the day in half hour shifts, we blew dry the wet patches. Even Mary and Sarah, who were reticent when it came to helping on the building site, offered to help. Our persistence paid off, and we salvaged the floor with minimal damage. We knew we'd been very lucky compared with the stories we'd heard, stories of frames collapsing and entire roofs ripped off in gale-force winds, of fires razing half-built houses to the ground. There would be no flood and no fire up at Voltaire's Garden. Not if I could help it.

Over three hundred millimetres of rain fall in three days, and by late February, warm, fresh, north-easterlies replaced the dry north-westerlies that had tormented the area through the drought. Some days were still hot, and I would sit on the cool concrete in the annex anticipating the next waft of air from the fan.

On one of those hot days, Mary and Sarah arrived home tired and grumpy from the heat. They went about their ritual of snacks and homework. For dinner, we ate salad from the produce freshly picked that day. After dinner, the air was still warm. Mary took a shower early before piano practice, and then Sarah took her turn, making her way back to their caravan in the dimming light.

In a few minutes she re-appeared, breathless.

'Mum, Greg, there's a cow eating grass by our caravan.'

'What!'

We exchanged glances. We knew where it had come from. It was an escapee from the ramshackle farm on the corner of the highway, owned by a spinster too old and too stubborn to adequately care for her fences. Her paddocks were overgrazed, her cattle hungry and tenacious. The surrounding properties endured the consequences with silent irritation, whilst keeping their gates closed. We tried to remember, but sometimes forgot to shut ours. By some miracle or just plain good luck, the cow had walked down the full length of our driveway, avoiding trampling all our baby trees and, ignoring the garden beds, orchards and vegies, headed straight for the lush grass on the transpiration bed beside the girls' caravan.

'I can't believe it,' Sarah went on, 'It was right by the door. Mary must have walked straight past it. How could she do that? Not see a cow?'

Greg and Sarah scrambled for shoes as I ran towards the caravan, slowing as I approached. I spotted the cow now behind the van munching grass. I shooed it back towards the fence, as Greg and Sarah approached from behind and bolted past me. They managed to steer it back up the driveway towards the gate, calling out and waving their arms.

As it got closer to the gate, the cow made a break for it, veering off towards the bottom of our ten-acre front paddock where more green grass grew on the banks of the water hole. It was not easy to chase a single cow in such a large paddock. Greg bolted one way and Sarah ran another, and it was then I noticed her surprisingly ungainly stride. It was not like her to run awkwardly. Still, she had good speed and coursed a wide circle to head off the cow.

I stood near the infirmary, ready to stop the cow from entering the gardens around the house. No sign of Mary. I could hear piano spilling from the caravan.

Greg and Sarah succeeded, and the cow walked sullenly back through the gate. They returned breathless.

'Where's Mary?' Sarah said.

'Still in there,' I pointed to the caravan.

Sarah opened the door, calling for her sister.

'What?' Mary snapped, miffed at the interruption.

'Didn't you hear us?'

'No.' Mary shook her head as if to say, why, should I have?

Sarah looked down at her feet and burst out laughing. She was wearing an old pair of Mary's canvas shoes, four sizes too big. No wonder she'd had so much trouble running.

A rural life was a natural life, and while cows normally belonged to farmers with good fences, other animals were free to roam wherever they liked. Knowing this, I was relieved it was the cow Sarah had noticed, and not the venomous if timid, four-foot long, red-bellied black snake we discovered under a stack of building material only two metres from the path to their caravan. It had moved there to feast on frogs, and we thought it was probably the same one that had shed its skin in the olive rips, the one we'd chased off the dam wall last spring. Greg had been happy to leave the snake alone but I made him chase it into next door's paddock. We moved the building materials and hadn't seen it since, but it left me feeling far from quiescent to life in the caravans.

One day in early March Greg and I stood inside the house in awe of its cavernous interior. It was the size of a small community hall. I imagined it left as it was. We could hold plays, concerts and public meetings, small indoor markets and school presentation nights. I pictured rows and rows of chairs and a stage at one end, a tea urn on an old table down one of the wings next to a small cake stand run by the ladies from the Country Women's Association, and someone seated at a table by the main door collecting the entrance fee and selling raffle tickets. There would be lamingtons and caramel slices, a perfect picture of Australian rural life.

'It's almost a shame to change it.' Greg said, echoing my thoughts.

'We could leave it like it is and pretend it's a warehouse.'

'Or have movable internal walls so that if we change our minds we can change the space.'

'Why would we bother? So much work and I'm so sick of moving anything, anywhere, and that includes walls.'

'You're right.' He took a fat stick of blue chalk from a tin perched on a noggin beside the front door. 'Come on, help me mark out the walls.'

We studied plans, made measurements and drew lines on the floor. He marked out the number of wall studs and, with a bit of jiggling here and there, we carved up half the interior space into three bedrooms, a small study and bathroom. The other half we turned into two large spaces with a four-metre partition wall between them, the living room to the south, the dining room and kitchen facing north.

It was hard to imagine each room in two dimensions on a plan or even on our chalky template. With each day that passed Greg erected another frame or two, one room and then another becoming a three-dimensional space. The interior wall frames made the area feel claustrophobic, and I began to wonder if our furniture would fit. I told myself I was succumbing to an illusion, but I used a tape measure, just to make sure.

Once the frames were up, I contacted the electrician and the plasterers. We were about to leap to the stage when rooms became habitable spaces. In preparation, the exterior walls needed insulating. To assuage my guilt over the floor and Greg's knees I refused his help, determined to do the whole house myself.

On another warm day I clothed myself in a long-sleeved shirt, thick pants, special disposable overalls, hat, sunglasses, paper mask and leather gloves and, with tape measure and Stanley knife in hand and perspiration already beading on my brow, I entered the building to face green bundles of vacuum-packed insulation. I felt ridiculous and I was melting. I cut the packaging and watched the bats inflate. They were bright yellow and smelled vaguely fishy. When I handled them itchy, prickly fibre-glass dust wafted into the air.

I knew I was not in for an easy time. Batts were sized according to standard building measurements, unlike the dimensions of our house. Taller than average ceilings meant we needed an extra row of noggins to support the wall studs, making each space in the walls shorter than the size of the standard batt. To make matters worse my love affair with tall thin windows had created another series of odd sized holes, each and every one of them needing to be filled with insulation. I grimaced when I stared at the external walls, and the hundreds of little holes to be filled.

I began by kneeling on the floor and carefully measuring and cutting a batt to fit, but after a few more carefully cut batts, I became impatient and decided to cut more by eye and less by measure. I filled cavity after cavity, wall by wall and room by room, up and down on my knees, back and forth with batts, until the whole space was clad in bright yellow fibreglass, smelling vaguely of fish.

The following Monday our plasterboard arrived, as did the plasterers, Tim and Mal. Unable to contain my excitement and wanting to watch the transformation, I fetched a folding canvas chair and plonked myself in the living room. It was not every day that you got to see your building become a home with smooth walls ready for painting. It was better than a movie and I wanted a ringside seat.

While I kicked back and admired the progress, agog at the frenetic pace the plasterers worked, Greg endured another hellish building task – insulating the ceiling. The plasterers were not keen to have the yellow bats hanging from the ceiling battens while they erected the plasterboard, since it inevitably meant faces full of fibre-glass. So instead, we agreed that Greg would lay bats on top of the plasterboard as they worked their way around the building. My role was to hand the batts up to him.

Only it didn't work out quite as planned. The plasterers were too fast. They put up sheet after sheet of plasterboard before Greg had a chance to catch up. Within half an hour he was stuck in the roof cavity, dressed for the Antarctic, with the autumn heat bearing down through the roof. The middle of the roof was fine, but when he needed to reach the low hips extending into the external corners of the building he had to shuffle across rafters, propelling himself into diminishing spaces using only the very tips of his toes with his body prostrate, while measuring, cutting and pushing bats ahead of him. It was a slow, tedious process, like a spider wasp dragging prey three times its size over rough terrain, and he needed all his determination and all his strength to do it.

I kept thinking of his poor knees.

Then I imagined Greg in one of his special places, his

euphemistic reference to those confined and precarious locations that arise when building. Special places included the tops of tall cupboards, the inside of cupboard carcasses and roof cavities.

At floor level, Tim and Mal joked and laughed mercilessly.

'Do you have rats in your roof?' Tim asked me. Or 'Everything all right up there?' he called out to Greg with a broad grin on his face.

For Greg it was a manic two days and he was glad when it was over. The fast pace, however, continued. Again, I was the cause, not wanting to spend another winter in the annex, especially with the girls at the age of fifteen. Not an easy year for a parent. I feared I'd not been paying them due attention, and I was concerned with Sarah's desire for a rich social life and Mary needing more room for her piano. Rearing teenagers was never easy, but on a building site it was no fun at all. In my eagerness for a house, I'd booked the plasterers a week prematurely, and that was the week Greg needed to prepare all the interior walls ready for plasterboard. Now he struggled to keep ahead.

The following afternoon, seated in my canvas chair, I watched Greg carry on his right shoulder a three-metre length of timber to the doorway that entered into the courtyard. He needed to cut it on the drop saw outside. A few days earlier, there were some concrete block steps below the doorway to accommodate the one-metre fall. We moved them yesterday, when we inserted the large, fixed pane window with the help of the plasterers. No one had thought to put the concrete blocks back under the French doors. Instead, Greg placed there a vinyl-covered stool with a fold out step.

I was seated in my canvas chair and Tim and Mal were in the hallway looking out of the smoked glass window as Greg's right foot touched the top of the stool.

We all watched, stunned, as the stool slipped from under his foot. His body lurched as he tried to steady the length of timber on his left shoulder. There was a loud thud and an even louder yowl as Greg fell sideways onto the clay pad below, narrowly avoiding knocking himself unconscious on more timber lying on the ground, and missing the sewer pipe that cut across the courtyard, his outstretched right arm breaking his fall. I rushed from my seat as he rose, unsteadily, clutching the top of his arm.

'I felt it bend,' he said weakly.

'You alright, mate,' Mal asked.

'You need to get to a doctor,' I said.

'I'll be fine.'

I didn't think he would be.

He gripped his arm, his face tense with pain as he climbed back into the house. There he began to tremble.

'Sit down,' I said, drawing the canvas chair towards him. 'Tea?'

'Okay.'

'You sure you don't want a doctor?'

Even after his fall, he refused to slow down. I couldn't fathom how he was managing to continue. He wouldn't see a doctor, and I knew he was feeling considerable pain. It kept him awake at night. He already had two damaged knees and now possibly a broken arm. His determination was almost absurd, like Monty Python's Black Knight, still wishing to fight as a limbless torso. His relentless efforts mirrored the pertinacity, the titanic struggles we had seen here in our garden: the one-legged plover struggling for food; the hawk with an injured wing trying to fly and succumbing to the persistent trampling of cows' feet; and the spider wasp that lost the prey it had painstakingly dragged across rough terrain to a marauding magpie.

I was worried about Greg. What was he trying to prove? He said he had no choice, but he did. He said he was working so hard to fulfil my desire for a house, but I would much rather have had a happy, uninjured husband. I feared the workload was making our lives unbalanced and, worse, Greg's state of mind too. Dave, Gino, Peter, they'd all tried to caution us against overdoing it. But we didn't listen. I was driven by a yearning to be off the dole and Greg, I had no clear idea of why he was driving himself so hard but it was starting to become clear to me that if he didn't steady his pace he was heading for a breakdown.

Greg struggled to retain his equanimity and apart from the occasional fractious moment, he managed quite well, although there were days when the girls and I called him 'grumpy drawers'. His spirit was Herculean and I could never have imagined it possible that someone more a dilettante than a builder, more a poet, wit, and incisive thinker than a labourer, could contain so much drive, so much strength and so much endurance.

CHAPTER FIVE

HOPE

"I had been looking forward,' said Pangloss, 'to a little discussion with you about cause and effect, the best of all possible worlds, the origin of evil, the nature of the soul, and pre-established harmony.'

At these words the dervish got up and slammed the door in their faces.'

CANDIDE

It was Maundy Thursday. We rose early and watched the sunrise bathe the mountains in glowing orange. It was my favourite time of year, when crystal-clear skies sharpened the skyline. I could distinguish individual trees, tracing in minute detail the subtle rises and falls of the mountains' contours in the ever-changing light.

Greg winced and rolled his shoulder.

'How's your arm?'

'The same.'

His reply was cryptic. I knew his pain was unrelenting. It was another sleepless night and, tired of his resistance to medical attention, this time, I wouldn't let it go.

'You have to get your arm and knees checked out. You can't go on like this. It's ridiculous. Will you let me make you an appointment?'

'It's only pain. What can a doctor do? I don't want operations and plaster casts. Where will that leave the building?'

'The building is not more important than your health. You need to find out what's wrong.'

'I know what's wrong, more or less.'

'Stop being an arrogant toad. You need to know for sure what the matter is. I need to know for sure. When we know, we can decide what to do, if anything. Will I make the call?'

'I'll go down the road and make an appointment myself. Thanks.'

Later, in the annex the dining table overflowed with bowls of tomatoes for bottling. While Greg sipped coffee, I sewed the final seam of the Aran cardigan I began knitting last winter, keen to have it finished before the next. After our second breakfast I would drive to Narooma to collect the floor sanders we hired for the Easter break. Looking at a very weary Greg over the mountain of red fruit, I couldn't believe he was prepared to use a sanding machine that day with his bad arm and knees. I winced recalling the floor sanding at his old house. He realised then why some jobs required heavy-set men with ballast. They could use body weight to control unwieldy power tools. Greg's light build meant he had to use muscle alone to manoeuvre the machine, muscles now joined to injured joints.

When I returned with the sanding machines, Greg donned overalls, a dust mask and sunglasses, and entered the house.

Hoping he didn't make his arm and knees worse, I took refuge in the annex away from the noisome whine, joining Mary and Sarah who were home from school.

An hour later, I went outside. The atmosphere was no longer sharp and clear. The smell of wood smoke stung my nose the moment I opened the door, and once I cornered the annex to look past Cobargo I was appalled to see the Wadbilliga mountains covered in a dense smoke haze. The wind was blowing from the south-west, carrying the smoke directly at us. They must have been doing a controlled burn, I thought. Every autumn the fire authority took advantage of the still cool air to conduct hazard reduction burns in the forests all around. I wished they didn't have to as it ruined the perfect weather. I didn't think the forest would ever burn around here in any case, not in a bushfire, although I had heard stories of a few fires in the area, but they were long ago in the 1950s. Maybe the warming climate had rendered this pocket of Australia less fire prone, not more. I had no idea.

My thoughts were interrupted when Greg staggered outside, no doubt hoping for fresh air, his body still vibrating by the look of him, and he was covered in dust. He replaced one kind of particulate pollution for another, a fresh, aromatic smell of Cyprus pine sawdust for the acrid odour of burning eucalypts.

'Can I do anything?' I said as he approached, hoping he didn't plan on going inside.

He didn't. He sat on the pew and stroked Pickles.

'A glass of water would be nice.'

Later in the day I read in the local paper that the smoke was not the result of a bushfire or the back-burning of tinder-dry undergrowth too easily lit by a match or a lightning strike. Instead, the burning was to germinate seed and stimulate new growth, part of a management regime designed to restore the national park to its former state, before it was logged. Yet I couldn't understand why those in charge decided to burn over Easter, the region's last tourist opportunity before the winter months, when families from Canberra, Melbourne and Sydney arrived to enjoy the pristine environment. In my view the timing of the act showed a lack of consideration for the tourism industry. I, for one, had not left the polluted atmosphere of central England to breathe bush smoke, and I was sure holidaymakers would feel the same.

My ill-informed thoughts would later be quashed by Greg in a single sentence: 'Climate change means far fewer days when the air is still enough to burn'.

Mary, showing signs of boredom, poked her head around the annex door and asked if she could use the Internet.

'What for?'

'I want to look up metal bands.'

It seemed pointless to argue, with the three of us feeling trapped inside by the smoke, and when I went back in I soon heard the girls through the caravan wall engrossed in cyberspace. I was less strict than Greg, who was vehemently opposed to surfing the net. He was anti-mobile phones, anti-Generation Y, and grew increasingly acerbic with two fifteen-year-old girls no longer willing to help us.

I empathised with the way they felt, forced to live a restricted lifestyle. Above all, life in the caravans restricted their social life.

Sleepovers here were just too much to contemplate and I put a limit on how far I was prepared to drive to drop off and collect. Sarah would spend whole weekends with her school friends from Bega High. And Mary would spend the night with Suzannah, whose parents had a vast mud-brick home they'd built in Dignam's Creek, or with Vanessa in Coolagolite, or with another friend Alice who was the closest. I never minded driving to collect Mary from Alice's as it meant catching up with her mother Gabrielle and enjoying the homey vibe of her mud-brick home cut into a grassy knoll on the edge of the forest. The land was a bush block, part of a subdivision of a local dairy farmer. You drove past the farm and across a creek to access the property. An attractive and confident woman with a mane of wavy blonde hair and a winning smile, Gabrielle was a community-minded artist who, among many other things, made fabulous baskets out of recycled material. Her husband Daniel was a talented potter and renowned kiln maker. They made for stimulating company and the views from their place looking west towards Peak Alone were stunning.

Visiting Gabrielle was respite. Tensions in the family were mounting. The only solution I could think of was to move into the house as soon as we could.

I gazed past the old gas cooker and through the large square window in the west wall to scan the horizon, seeing smoke and imagining fiercely hot flames flickering above trees. I found it terrifying to imagine Wadbilliga ablaze. A wild, rugged place of deep river gorges, skeletal ridges, precipitous cliffs, dense bush and towering trees. Its thirty-four thousand hectares included the Brogo Wilderness, acknowledged as the largest pristine river catchment under the control of the National Parks and Wildlife Service in New South Wales. Much of Wadbilliga was old-growth forest. While vast tracts of forest in the region were clear-felled last century, the inaccessibility of Wadbilliga saved much of it from the saw. When I recalled reading on a website that it was home to one hundred and twenty-two species of native bird, along with wombats, echidnae, possums, platypi, swamp wallabies and the eastern grey kangaroo, I shuddered at the prospect of so much death out there just now and hoped the firies knew what they were doing and the animals could all escape the fire.

It was a tragedy inherent to the native Australian habitat that in our changing climate it ignited too easily; burned too hot and fast. When in drought, this corner of Australia suffered from perpetual sunshine, dry air, searing temperatures and winds that blew like fire themselves. Greg told me in extreme conditions volatile eucalyptus oil hovered above the tree canopy, an explosive floating bubble poised to transmute into a fireball, that hot winds can fan flames to heights of fifty metres, that fires travel at frightening speeds, razing homes and towns in seconds, transforming a bucolic paradise into a smouldering wasteland. But not in Cobargo. No, no, that was not possible. That sort of thing never happened in the Bega Valley.

I might have complained about back-burning, but I knew there was no choice. Perhaps Australia was designed to burn and all we could do was manage it, both the fires and our relationship with the land, just as indigenous Australians had always done. They had special ways with fire to manage their country.

Maybe fire was inevitable and as a nation we would continue to face the horror of fire in the dry parts of the continent, those areas away from the moist sea breezes that lessened the fire risk, like the Canberra fires of January 2003.

Watching smoke billowing on the horizon I was taken back to that January weekend. Greg and I had driven down to Burragate, a locality some hundred kilometres south, to celebrate my birthday. We stayed for a few days in a rustic, mudbrick dwelling in the middle of farmland and bush. It was owned by Jim-at-the-pool, who let us stay for our first, and so far only romantic getaway, but we went the weekend of the Canberra fires. Thick smoke reduced the horizon to a few hundred metres in every direction. The sky stayed orange all day, lit by a dim, red disk. The landscape was yellowy-brown and dry. In the foreground tea trees and wattles looked eerie, their wizened branches silhouetted against the smoke haze. Behind them the landscape was murky. If it weren't for the smell, I might have imagined fog, not smoke, but my sinuses stung from the odour of burning wood laced with overtones of eucalyptus. It was an apocalyptic scene, even in Burragate, two hundred kilometres from the fire ground.

Today I remained indoors with the windows closed tight. In my mind I saw smoke from fires everywhere, not just that of the controlled burns in Wadbilliga. Farmers were burning stubble to encourage more vigorous growth next season, and people were disposing of garden debris, pruning clippings and goodness knows what else in backyard burn-offs in the village. I remembered flying over the tropical rainforests of Ghana, where farmers slashed and burned. We were making the descent into Accra at night, and below I could see many bright-reddish lights flickering in the blackness, each one a fire.

Fire is as natural as water, earth or air; it is nature's incendiary way of transforming one thing into another. After all, the Aboriginal peoples lit fires as farming practice, to startle animals from the bush, burn dead trees, open up savannah and germinate seed. Yet the actions of so many humans now living on the planet had created a grave imbalance in the natural world. Humanity had not only muddied nature's waters through pollution, ravaged the earth through mining and farming, and fouled the air with a plethora of chemicals, we were rapacious for fire: fires for fuel, fires for electricity, fires for heat, for food, for industry. I was a superstitious soul and as one old friend so often said to me, 'what goes around comes around'. And it would. I was sure of it. Which was why I'd moved to an idyllic location far from all the nonsense of modern life, safe in the knowledge that we would be supported by the land in our sustainable lifestyle adventure.

Collectively we know the damage fires do to the earth's

atmosphere, we know that carbon dioxide and other greenhouse gas emissions are killing the planet. We know, but do we change? No.

It was in such moments that my hope for a better world was small. I tried not to feed a sense of horror at the blindness we humans displayed towards an irrefutable and absolute necessity for change. I wanted to believe that humankind was a higher evolutionary being adept at adaptability, yet too many human-lit fires confronted me; their existence symbolising inertia, immobility, and a fixity of thinking and acting that boded no good.

It was difficult to keep hope alive inside my heart when the world around me did little to justify having such hope. It was easy to keep hold of hope in the face of temporary, fixable troubles, those I could influence and change. How much harder it was when I faced more enduring problems caused by others who refused to change their ways. Or when I heard on the radio that governments wanted us all to use energy efficient light globes. Will reducing our use of the light globe solve our voracious appetite for power consumption, when the home computer draws as much electricity as a fridge? As if the cause of global warming was a morbid fear of darkness that had us switching on every light globe we could lay our hands on. After all, no harm in turning them off. If only we could shine that light upon ourselves and examine the rest of our behaviour more closely.

Sarah called to me from behind the caravan door.

'What is it?'

'I want one of these.' She beckoned me into the office caravan and pointed to the screen. A lurid pink dress with an expensive price tag beamed back at me.

'No.'

I slammed the door behind me before the inevitable pestering began.

Humanity runs on impulse. We create grooves with our thoughts and our actions and these grooves deepen the more we travel down them. Trapped inside the gullies and gorges of our own making, we lose sight of alternatives and easily become lost. To avoid becoming entrenched perhaps we needed to follow the ridge-lines on higher ground, allow a part of us to hover above, step outside, transcend, reflect, evaluate, then act, with a good sense of direction, as moral beings. Elevated thoughts, and after spending three doctoral years immersed in metaphysical thought, I didn't believe there was much to be gained by seeking explanations, causes or solutions for the difficult or cataclysmic situations we create by turning to metaphysics either. God was not going to save us from the ruination we persisted in pursuing. Even if a creator God made this, the best of all possible worlds, we still had the capacity to ruin it with our apparent free will. I questioned how free our will was, though, if we were unable to change it.

Sometimes, on days such as this, I struggled to keep hold of hope. I knew that without it, pessimism, depression or despair would enter my being, just as it touched Candide in his melancholic moments. He is often depicted as a naïve idealist, yet he also portrays resilience, and it was this quality of endurance that was tested in me. It is the will-to-hope that bolsters hope, energises optimism and feeds life, not death: Eros, not Thanatos. Hope forges on when things seem grim, hope makes an effort in spite of adversity.

Hope meant picking myself up no matter how low I felt and doing something positive even though a large part of me had no desire to do so. Hope led me forward, despair took me backwards, hope lifted me out of myself, despair locked me deep within my own misery. Hope had a directional quality, it pointed to the future, not the past. It was hope I needed, and sometimes I saw it glued to the bottom of Pandora's box.

The fires burned out and the wind carried the smoke away about the same time that Greg finished sanding and he finally took himself to the doctor. A series to tests revealed he'd torn some cartilage in his knee, which would require surgery, but there was nothing to be done about his baker's cyst or his aching arm, neither requiring intervention of any kind.

It was now my turn to be busy on the building. The house was ready to paint. I was so excited I turned into a whirlwind with a paintbrush. I chose a colour palate similar to Voltaire's first retreat at Les Délices. He had chosen greens, reds and yellows. For the interior, I selected soft greens, a deep red, a creamy yellow and raw umber. I applied Tung oil to the floors and they turned to honey and shone.

I was so keen to move in to our home after a year in the caravans I worked like fury, so hard in fact, that I lost six kilos. My already thin body looked emaciated. My hipbones stuck out and my face looked gaunt. Size eight pants needed a belt and worse, I had become flat-chested. I knew I was risking burning out again; it wasn't the first time since I left England that I'd driven myself in this way on the wings of my own desire to get things done. After submitting my thesis, I spent a week in bed in a kind of grey dog depression. I never wanted to go there again. Yet I exercised no restraint. None whatsoever. If I continued this way now, the message my body was giving me was clear, I'd disappear.

I slowed down one day in early May, after moving the contents of our bedroom caravan into the house. It was the first night in our new home, and I was enjoying the contrast from the confines of the caravans. It felt glorious if strange to find myself ensconced in a large bedroom, with the polished Cyprus floor, the soft green walls and lovely silk curtains of dark bluish purple I'd made from lengths of fabric I scored in a charity shop. Our bed in the middle of the room looked small, and I could walk around it and get out from either side. I felt like hopping in and out for a while just for fun. Instead, I lay on my back beside Greg feeling like an over-exposed mouse.

'You don't think it's too big, do you?' It was always me that had the anxious thoughts.

'Not at all,' Greg said, a little too firmly.

'What about the wall colour? Do you like it?'

'I never thought green would work but it does. I like it very much.'

I stared up, wide-eyed.

'The ceiling is so far away.'

'Sh.' He turned on his side facing away from me and promptly fell asleep.

At least our nightmares would pass. In the caravans we both had dreams of super-highways and landing strips cutting a course through our garden, of out-of-control dump trucks ploughing into the building site, of developers planning a gargantuan housing estate on the land next door.

The following morning, I got up and threw open the curtains to let the sunlight stream through our north-facing windows.

'You got the passive-solar heating thing just right,' Greg said, shielding his eyes.

He rolled over on his side, enjoying the warmth. I turned back to the window.

Our bedroom overlooked the top terrace and I couldn't help but see more work to do. I knew I should be admiring the mountains beyond, but my gaze settled on the weeds. It didn't take long for a garden to turn into a weedy mess. It had been our challenge all along, both of us torn between building a home and creating a garden.

Not all the weeds were unwanted. There were self-seeded lettuces popping up in cracks between low rock walls, on embankments and in lawn. But the weeds were threatening to consume the terraces again, and the paddock needed mowing. Most important of all, I had to plant up the terraces with winter vegetables.

After a hurried breakfast in the annex, leaving Greg to get on with building the kitchen cupboards, I headed straight outdoors, relishing time in the fresh air after weeks inhaling paint fumes. I located my trowel and made my way to the terraces. I was pleased to find a hardy variety of spinach self-seeding like the lettuces. The snow peas I'd managed to plant amidst the painting were doing well and there were still some tomatoes ripening despite the cooler weather. Aside from those few vegetables, the terraces look bedraggled.

On the top terrace, I stood beside a clump of weeds, my stainless-steel trowel with its rubberized, blue handle in my hand, ready to separate plant life from the soil it clung to. I loved gardening. Like swimming it brought me to a state of peace with the world. My mood changed the moment I knelt and soon I was like a child in a sea of dirt, surrounded by the minutiae of life. I uncovered a host of insects and nematodes at work. I saw slugs and snails harbouring under bits of fallen bark; wolf spiders darting out of homes and running for cover; witchetty grubs all white, juicy and plump; slaters, millipedes, beetles and crickets; and worms that wriggled in the burning sunshine before I buried them again to save their life. When I paused for a rest, I looked up, savouring the tremendous view. I had the two ends of the scale right here, landscape and soil, the whole and its parts. I had the whole of life in front of me and little else mattered.

As for the weeds, they were life too, life in the wrong location, for us. And what weeds! Tussocky paddock grasses like paspalum with its dense root ball that gripped the soil like a vice and always seemed to grow directly beside the base of other plants, making its removal a precarious operation. Paspalum squeezed out the competition like a supersized thug taking up more than its share of the bus seat, sandwiching you between its great bulk and the window. Then there were the weeds that sent out runners that were even worse than the tussocks. They strangled the roots and stems of competitors. I thrust the trowel into the soil ahead of me, where a cluster of asparagus was entangled by couch grass, with its trifid nodules and deep wiry runners that snapped off somewhere underground when I tried to pull them out. Among this tangle, sheep's sorrel had produced a mat of runners a few inches deep, sending down occasional woody roots deep into the sub-soil, roots impossible to remove without digging crater-sized holes.

To my left was a mat of kikuyu, the peregrine king of the weed empire, a heavy-duty, grass runner from Kenya, so named in 1903 after the indigenous inhabitants of the East African highlands. It was introduced in Australia in 1919 on a farm in Tilba Tilba, twenty kilometres north, as an experiment in pasture improvement. Kikuyu has thick, tenacious runners traveling above and below ground. Greg said it took four years to establish itself in Tilba, after which the grass became prolific. Kikuyu loved clay, and appeared like magic in any soil disturbed by digging. Kikuyu runners have been known to tunnel under two-lane highways, and this remarkable ability had given rise to the longest kikuyu runner category at the Cobargo Agricultural Show. It was great for lawns of course, but a nuisance elsewhere, out-competing native grasses.

The weeds pulled free more easily on the terraces, only the couch and kikuyu gave me trouble, and in ten minutes I had a barrowful to dump in the orchard. Greg called it 'trash mulching', quoting his guru, Louis Bromfield. We used trash mulch to build new garden beds on ground where the topsoil was thin or non-existent, and we found it worked very well; dead weeds rot fast.

Weeding and trash mulching helped to re-organise nature's randomness, creating human-inspired order from apparent chaos. Gardening was always a partnership with nature, placing a human stamp in accordance with some pragmatic or utilitarian purpose, but always with an aesthetic sense, an eye for beauty that embraces what pre-exists in a landscape. I thought of gardens as ongoing works of art; and gardening as a continuous creative process that drew us compulsively into a world outside of ourselves. Every gardener was an artist, working in the language of the earth, and the wages were life, beauty and sustenance.

On my way back to the terraces with my empty barrow, I noticed clouds building over the mountains and in an hour my weeding was curtailed by rain. I loved the rain at any time, but for Greg, it meant drainage work to prevent the downpour from pooling under the house or running down the hillside too quickly, leaving subsoil dry and causing erosion. Greg was keen to redirect our rainwater flows, steering them away from places requiring dry ground, and into soaks, rubble drains and swales, slowing stormwater flow to enable good absorption into the soil. It was about drought-proofing and deluge management.

When the rain eased to a light drizzle, I couldn't resist the outdoors. I tidied some building materials strewn on the embankment behind the caravans watching Greg scooping clay mud from one of his drainage channels.

'What do you think?' he asked as I walked by. He stood back all proud.

'Looks great. What next?'

'I'm going to do the same to the house,' he called back, already on his way.

Greg's drainage work began behind the caravans and shed, flowing into a pipe in a trench to take the flow towards the house, then redirected via a swale to make a detour around the house piers towards another trench on the high side of the orchard that would soon become a rubble soak. He then directed the water around the third rainwater tank we'd put in place at the end of the orchard to capture the rainwater running off the west wing. The house was split level and the western side too low to drain into the main tank. I was disappointed we'd had to locate the tank in front of the dam, obscuring the natural beauty in the views from the house, but we had to be practical. Besides, the orchard would obscure the tank soon enough.

A second shovel leaned against the laundry wall. I couldn't resist it. I scraped and watched rivulets swirl, eddy and flow. Mini-dams emerged as silt banked up behind a pebble. I scraped again. Only I'd scraped too deeply and the water began to pool. It wasn't as easy as it first appeared to create a smooth flow, but it was fun; I was a child again, remembering the fun I used to have with toy excavators, building roads on gravel driveways, playing sticks and stones with bare feet in puddles.

A week later, the rain had gone and the wind had dried out the ground. I looked out the living room windows at the driveway, expecting Jack and Carolyn's car to appear at any moment. Greg had been keen since Christmas to show Voltaire's Garden to his mother, and now that were living in the house, it was an opportune moment. Jack had popped in a few times in the last year, but Carolyn, frail and unsteady on her feet, had only visited once, when we were still in the caravans.

A car slowly coursed its way down the driveway. I moved from the window and called to Greg, who then appeared on the front lawn ready to help his mum out of the car. Mary and Sarah joined me in the kitchen. I put the kettle on. Soon there was chatter and exclamations as Greg showed his mum around the house.

His parents were full of praise as we sat and chatted over tea and cake – a rustic apple and date slice. Jack was keen to look at the garden so I took him for a walk, leaving the others indoors. We walked to the terraces to admire the vegetables, strolling between beds, me pointing and picking and offering him smells. Then a noise from behind caused me to turn. I nudged Jack's arm.

My little red car was heading slowly towards us across the lawn, narrowly avoiding trees, shrubs and garden beds. Carolyn sat in the passenger seat like a petite queen, wearing enormous sunglasses and a big smile. Jack laughed and I laughed with him, pleased that Greg had found a way to show the results of all our hard work so far to the most important woman in his life other than me: his mother. She wasn't a gardener and she had little idea of the work involved, but she was a woman of taste and an appreciator of beauty, and her approval was important to him and would no doubt bring him joy.

Before they left I filled a bag with produce, loving the appreciative comments from Jack as I handed him the bag. We'd never needed to seek Jack's approval; we were living a life he too would have loved. Greg and I had his approval for another reason. We worked with all the organisation, diligence and strategic planning worthy of a logistics officer's respect. Or rather, I did. Greg, who liked to do 'the next thing', which was a euphemism for what took his fancy, felt strait jacketed by my regimentation.

I inherited those qualities from my mother, who used them

most efficaciously each time she moved house. A few days later she visited, this time to say farewell. My parents had sold their farm to a couple from Canberra a few months earlier, and had purchased a new house in Bega, forty-five kilometres south. We hugged and exchanged kind words.

'I'll still get my hair cut in Cobargo,' she said.

'And I'll visit when I shop in Bega,' I replied.

The exchange was brief. Sadness welled in my heart. I would be seeing a lot less of her. I barely left Cobargo and when I did I went north to Narooma for Mary's piano lesson and the supermarket and sometimes to Greg's parents. I sensed the rift that had been present ever since I threw in my lot with Greg deepening a little bit more.

Winter, and after breakfast one chilly July morning, I stoked the fire in our cavernous living room before opening the curtains on a heavy frost blanketing the landscape in shimmering white. A thick band of mist filled the valley, the iron rooftops of Cobargo protruding like a succession of mutely coloured hats, and above the mist, the mountain forests were bathed in the orange light of dawn.

And, halfway along the driveway, there was Greg. He had a wheelbarrow with a rake and hoe stacked against it. He appeared to be digging with a post-hole shovel and hurling the dirt into the rips on the high side.

What was he up to now?

I put on a beanie, warm leather gloves, two pairs of socks and a thick winter jacket, and I walked up the driveway to find out.

'Hey,' I called as I neared him. 'Another project?'

Greg leaned on his shovel.

'I'm digging a dish drain.'

'A ditch drain?'

'A dish drain. Like a plate only deeper.'

'And longer by the look of it.'

I cast my eyes along the length of the driveway. This was some task he'd taken on. Any normal person would have used machinery. But Greg wasn't normal. He was eccentric, a touch bizarre and if he could do a task the hard way, he would.

A few weeks earlier we had ordered more gravel to improve the driveway. It was expensive and Greg wanted to make sure it would last. He'd worked on roads before so he knew what to do. A dish drain on the high side would funnel water into a pipe that went under the driveway at the lowest point and down towards the front dam.

But we had three hundred metres of driveway.

Greg carefully removed the top soil beside the gravel and hurled it into the rips as fill. When he reached sub-soil and clay he barrowed it to the other side of the road to fill any dips and help prevent the gravel from washing down the hill. Not only would the whole process protect our investment in road base, it would also mean we harvested more water on our land, making it flow into our water hole in the south-facing paddock, instead of out the gate and down the road.

'Can I help?' I wondered how, but I couldn't leave him alone with such a gargantuan task.

Greg handed me a post-hole shovel.

'Just follow the slope I've made. I'll shovel the clay down here.'

The ground was soft from winter rain. The shovel sliced through the earth with ease. Greg observed my method.

'Just make sure you don't go too deep.'

'It's okay. I'm getting the hang of it.'

Satisfied, he took a hoe and rake to the pile of clay sods he'd barrowed earlier.

My spade and shovel work had improved greatly over the last year. I established a rhythm and continued until I was too hungry to lift another shovel full of earth. I looked at my watch and found a whole hour had passed in what seemed like five minutes, and he was still hoeing sods. I couldn't bear the thought of him hoeing and raking all that soil and clay down both sides of the driveway alone.

'Second breakfast?'

As we strolled back to the house, I suggested a trip to the hardware store.

I was ready to transcend my dependence on the humble trowel and my recent mastery of the fork and shovel. I was about to embrace the hoe.

At the hardware store I bought a sturdy, hand-forged chipping hoe, flexing my muscles and scoffing to myself as I walked past a stand of 'tools for women' sporting pink and purple plastic handles.

In the afternoon, after Greg had stopped building, we returned to the dish drain. I stood before a pile of sods in the rips and tried out my new hoe. At first, I found the action awkward and difficult, but after several failed attempts I hurled the hoe into a sod and it sliced through it like a spoon in custard. I did it again and again, swinging the hoe over one shoulder, taking aim, and letting it fall. Remembering to swap sides, I raised it over the other shoulder. Muscles I never knew existed made their presence felt, protesting feebly. Ignoring the twinges, I hoed and hoed and hoe some more, triumphant. I was so proud! I now had an opportunity to be of significant help to Greg. His workaholic craziness was contagious.

He got lonely working on the building every day, and my presence on the driveway seemed to return him to his normal cheery self. I worked quietly, concentrating on my efforts, while he burst into song, recalling snatches from his 1950s childhood, filling my ears with tunes from *Porgy and Bess*. He continued with a rendition of *Old Man River* that had me in awe, my little Slovenian man singing with the rich, deep, throaty voice of Paul Robeson. He finished with *Puff, the Magic Dragon* and an odd mixture of American military songs he learned as a child.

Done with singing he entertained me with his standard diatribe on cheap factory products designed to break on first use, screws that sheered off at the slightest twist, tools too fragile for hardwood, and nails that bent under the hammer, as compared to the virtue and simplicity of my hand-forged hoe with its hardwood handle.

I remained silent, half listening, half in my own thoughts, pleased.

We committed ourselves to an hour or two on the dish drain each morning at dawn and, after lighting the fire and preparing dinner early and leaving both in the care of Mary and Sarah, I joined him for another hour at dusk. It was a genial time for us. I appreciated the things Greg saw and heard – a bird in the sky, a cloud, an interesting rock, or an unusual insect – and he took enormous delight in my appreciation of the views.

Taking short breaks, we would stand together and admire the landscape. It was unavoidable when the morning mists were sublime, the atmosphere so clear and crisp. At dawn, and again at dusk, the sky filled with mellow pinks and peaches. We could see the enfolding ridges of Peak Alone and Narira Mountain to our north. The ridges on Peak Alone look like crossed arms covered in a green woolly blanket of trees embracing the steep-sided gullies in the mountain's lap. The low light angles of early morning and evening revealed more shapes and contours in Wadbilliga. Every time I looked I saw something new. I was fascinated by the continual changes in the panorama, brought about by the changes in light and in my location. Sometimes I captured a contour in my gaze, only to find it gone when I looked again; the light had moved, the definition lost.

Each evening we walked back to the house under an eastern sky swathed in muted violet.

One evening, on the porch I turned to find the western sky glowing warm orange. Greg joined me.

'Look.'

He pointed across the lawn.

Pickles emerged from the rips and was sauntering towards us, clutching a droopy grey body in her jaws.

'Not so close young Pick's,' I called out. As if she heard, Pickles flopped down a few metres from our feet to eat her kill: a mouse.

'It's the rips,' Greg said. 'This morning, a mouse bolted across my feet and dived into one. I think all our mulching has provided a haven for rodents.'

'Which explains the hawk on the fence post yesterday.'

'You saw it too?'

'From the windows. It flew over to Hawk's Nest Ridge.'

'No kidding? Hey, I bet the mice are fertilising our trees. They drag all kinds of food stuffs and bedding down into their burrows, and then there are the droppings.'

It was true. The rips started out as a mess of dishevelled clods. Three-tyne rips meant ours were three times worse. By hoeing the clods, top dressing with spare soil and mulching half a metre thick, we'd tamed them without compacting the earth back into impenetrability. In the process we'd created a subterranean paradise, a habitat for mice, lizards, crickets, and even the occasional snake.

· · ·

We hadn't seen Charlie or his timber for weeks. We left messages on his phone but he hadn't replied. Greg insisted he was just busy with his winter cycle of fencing and firewood orders, but it didn't prevent me from worrying. We needed his timber for the internal walls of the B&B rooms and I began to wonder whether I could manage to persuade Greg that pine would do as an alternative. I was bracing myself to do just that when Charlie pulled into our driveway late one afternoon with a cheeky smile and a load of timber.

'G'day Isobel, how's things?' he asked, untying his dog.

'All the better for seeing you Charlie.'

I looked around to see if Greg would appear to help unload. He didn't.

'What've you been up to Charlie?' I said. 'We thought we'd never see you again.'

'Ah sorry, mate. First I got that bloody 'flu. Set me back two weeks, it did, and then I nearly lost the ute.'

'Oh no! How?'

He reached into the cabin for a cigarette and then, fortified by a sharp inhale of his smoke, he told us he'd been in the bush milling timber behind Puen Buen, where Patto and Gino lived. He'd loaded the ute with sleepers and his scraggy dog, and was ready to head home for a beer, only to find he had a flat battery.

'I chained the ute to the skidder to haul it up the hill for a clutch start, but the ute got away and headed back down the gully into the bush with me dog on the back tray.'

'What happened?' I said, glancing down at his dog.

'It gets worse. I killed the skidder motor and jumped off to chase the ute, but I forgot the handbrake, didn't I, and the bloody skidder headed off towards me spot mill. Jeez I was lucky. The skidder managed to miss every tree on the way down and stopped against a pile of rubbish. But the bloody ute, it's bouncing down the gully between the trees, and then it sort of rears up on its back wheels, and there's sleepers flying everywhere, and the poor old dog bouncing around. I swear to God, you couldn't have driven it down there without hitting something. It finally pulled up against a sapling, with one sleeper and the dog still on the back, every panel dented, the bull bar ripped off and the windscreen cracked. Had to take a sledge hammer to it to straighten it out a bit before I could drive it home.'

The way he recounted the near catastrophe, it was hard to know whether to roar with laughter or offer my sympathy.

'Thank goodness you're all right, Charlie.'

'Yeah. I'm all right. Sorry it's taken me so long to get here, but.'

'It's just good to see you.'

I leaned against his ute as untied the ropes. Something about Charlie got under my skin. Maybe he reminded me of my paternal Cockney heritage; he had the same flashness. I had an image of uncles standing by the Christmas tree telling cor blimey tales, me a little girl listening agog to her grandad's First World War stories in the Khyber Pass.

Charlie heaved the timber off his ute, dumping it on the ground nearby in a heap. It came to me to ferry that timber down to the west wing. The arrival of more timber meant Greg could finish the guest rooms. It was September, sixteen months since we'd moved into the caravans and there was still an enormous workload ahead of us. It would be another year at least before Greg could tell himself the building was finished and turn his attention to garden infrastructure, such as our much-desired propagating shed and chicken coop.

Meanwhile, I'd found another job. I had foregone sorting mail at the post office to be personal assistant to literary agent Mary Cunnane, who'd relocated from further up the coast. Mary had worked as vice president and senior editor for a top publishing house in New York, before going into what I presumed was semi-retirement. I knew nothing about publishing and even less about literary agents but this was much needed part time work, conveniently located in the coastal town of Bermagui, about twenty minutes drive, and it meant we were no longer on the dole. I worked short hours four days a week. I started at ten and was home by four thirty, allowing me plenty of time at either end of each day to mow lawns, tend the garden, do the housework and deal with anything Mary and Sarah needed of me. Plenty of time, but I was already worked off my feet.

Mary Cunnane added to my workload by encouraging me to write a memoir of Voltaire's Garden. Every Friday she would ask me if I would be writing that weekend and every Tuesday she wanted a progress report. Suddenly, I was having a stab at being an author.

The Saturday after Charlie appeared was scheduled to be a great leap forward; we were laying a seven-metre square concrete slab in the courtyard, covering the sewer pipe Greg nearly fell on the day he hurt his arm. In the early morning light, I noted for the last time the clay fill, half a metre deep and retained by a concrete-block wall. I had barrowed all that clay there day after day from the huge clay pile that had been sitting beside the rainwater tank, barrows one third full with heavy lumps of moist clay I'd hacked off the pile with a mattock, and then tamped down using Greg's home-made whacky packer, a pole nailed to a chunk of Oregon pine. I didn't barrow *all* the clay, Greg helped, but I still felt triumphant. Hard physical labour was satisfying, or so I thought. By then, I'd absorbed Greg's ways and become his female doppelganger. When really, the job could have been done in an hour with a back hoe.

My reverie was interrupted by the arrival of Gino, who was as adept with concrete as he was with roof trusses. He brought his son Clyde, and together with our friend and local musical talent Damon Davies, along with several old wheelbarrows, the concrete moving could begin. The cement truck arrived on schedule, parking beside the garage at the front of the house, with the five cubic metres of concrete that needed to be barrowed across uneven ground to the courtyard around the back. Unlike the back hoe, the concrete truck had no access around the back of the house. I knew the process from when we poured the footings. We had the same volume of concrete and there was always the panic that the concrete would go off in the truck. It was painfully arduous work and there was little I could do other than watch as barrow after barrow came hurtling down the slope and the contents tipped onto the clay.

Two hours of intense, gruelling work later, all the men were hungry, thirsty, sweaty and dusty. I went out the front and saw Greg and Damon cleaning tools by the annex, clearly in desperate need of refreshment. I disappeared back into the house to prepare them a second breakfast.

When I placed before Greg and Damon, who were seated on the pew, a tray containing a large plate of little Scotch pancakes – pikelets – a bowl of fresh strawberry compote and another of homemade yogurt, along with a pot of Earl Grey tea, they were dumbstruck.

'Tuck in,' I urged taking a pancake for myself.

'What a breakfast,' Damon said, diving in.

'It's part of the breakfast menu for our guests.'

'Book me in, this is delicious.'

'Where's Gino?' I said, seeing he was missing.

'He's still on the slab with the float, he won't be joining us.'

'And Clyde?'

'Gone home.'

'More for us then. Terrific.'

Damon took another pikelet laden with topping. Greg was

already on his third. I left them to it and went back inside the house.

Two hours later, I found Gino cleaning his float. He'd missed out on the pancake feast as he couldn't leave the slab. I took in the smooth grey mass drying in the sun. He'd done an excellent job, they all had.

'Time for a beer?' he said, adding, 'It's the tradition. Lay a slab, have a beer.'

I didn't need persuading. I went and found Greg.

'Shall we celebrate the slab with a beer? It's Gino's idea.'

'It's the tradition,' Gino said, walking up behind us.

'Alright then,' said Greg. He didn't sound that enthusiastic. Alcohol wasn't his thing. 'I guess it's me who goes to get it.'

When he returned we went and sat on the guest wing's veranda to salute the day's efforts. The veranda overlooked Wadbilliga and now that the view was no longer blocked by the girls' caravan – which Patto and Gino had bought – as I drank my long neck of stout, my eyes followed the contours of Dumpling Ridge.

'This view really does something to me.' I paused. 'I can't explain it.'

'It's not the view, it's the place,' Gino said. 'You can visit anyone around here and each time the scenery is different, the house is different and the people are different, but in the end it's the same. We are all doing the same thing.'

I thought about that for a while. There *was* a strong sense of community here, among those born into the area and the blow ins from elsewhere; no-one I'd encountered here wasn't touched by the exquisite landscape, but Gino was referring to a sense of place as a whole, including its people. Which was different to the aesthetic feelings I experienced when beholding the mountains.

I stared at the view of Wadbilliga again. The more I looked, the more I learned of its layers of ridges and gullies, curves and cliffs, and the more I felt consumed by it. When I'd bought this land my sense of ownership extended to the perimeter fence, but the view had drawn me beyond, pulling me into its farthest reaches. Now the land for me was not this land or that land, but what I could see from where I stood. I derived a deep sense of place from the environs. It was, I supposed, a spiritual connection. When I was absorbed by the view we had of Wadbilliga, I was lifted out of my mundane world, transported into a realm of beauty, beholding, contemplating in awe, wonder and appreciation. It was a deeply intimate experience, a feeling of closeness, yet I was transported beyond myself, as if *I* didn't matter, and my worries, thoughts, emotions and desires disappeared for a while. I was simply a pair of eyes, looking.

I was curious, too, to understand the view's topography. On a shopping trip to Bega the other week I'd purchased four topographical maps. I needed four to cover the whole area. Once home I laid them out on the living room floor, with their adjoining edges aligned. Satisfied, I kneeled and stared, puzzling over contours and distances, my knowledge of topographical map reading scant.

I found the mountains easy to recognize because the contour lines were shaped in increasingly smaller concentric shapes. When a mountain was more a series of ridges and gullies with no identifiable peak, it grew difficult to imagine the formation in three dimensions. I was familiar with Peak Alone, the cone-shaped mountain to our northwest, nearly a thousand metres high, with long arms folded in its lap, looking like a seated monk shrouded in robes with its head bowed in prayer. Peak Alone was situated to the north-west, and divided Wandella from Yowrie, two farming localities in Cobargo's hinterland. Tracing my finger along the large, forested hills forming the northern horizon across our dam, I identified Sam's

Ridge and Narira Mountain, part of the Bodalla State Forest. On and behind them, a network of dirt roads and tracks followed the ridges. When I looked closely, I could see that every ridge had a track or a road, most of them logging tracks, the complexity too confusing for a city navigator used to orienting by man-made landmarks, like buildings. It was a recipe for getting lost.

Tracking along the closest ridgeline to the west, behind which were several more layers of ridges and mountains before the escarpment of the Great Dividing Range, I found Mount Dumpling, another cone-shaped peak of around five-hundred metres, almost due west of us. Mount Dumpling captured the eye and the imagination, like a peaked hat worn by a small child sitting in the front row of an audience; it appeared youthful and cheeky, positioned beside several heavy-set adults.

My crouched body stiffened. I stood up. Leaning beside the pair of west-facing dining room windows I studied the prospect in relation to the maps. Mount Dumpling was framed by two stands of trees in the foreground and behind it the mountains receded to the escarpment in the distance.

I returned to the maps. Tracking south from Mount Dumpling I found lumpy Dumpling Ridge, which was eclipsed at its southern end by Hawk's Nest Ridge which merged into Murrabrine Mountain, more a sprawling ridge of around three kilometres than an actual peak. Excited at these discoveries I returned to the maps and looked further into Wadbilliga National Park. At first, I was impressed by the absence of roads and tracks on the ridgelines, dotted orange lines that made it easier to recognize the topology. I tracked the blue lines of the creeks and rivers, imagining I was in gullies looking up at ridges, the red contour lines packed tightly together in many places, indicating steep slopes. The rivers and creeks had names – Little Creek, Lake Creek, Queens Pound River – but most of the ridges and peaks were nameless – I could only find Sunday Hill and Wadbilliga Mountain in around fourteen kilometres square.

Wadbilliga Mountain, at one thousand, three hundred and thirty-eight metres, a figure I quoted so often I would never forget it, was the highest peak in the area. It had a Trig point – whatever that was – and a fire trail passing nearby, and it had some topological significance. It was the source of the Wadbilliga and Brogo Rivers, the latter supplying the Brogo Dam: Cobargo's water supply.

I left the maps and headed outside, keen to match my abstract discoveries to reality. I wanted to be sure that the peak I could see in the distance, just to the north of Mount Dumpling, was Wadbilliga Mountain and not one of the nameless peaks in between. With a sixteen-kilometre distance between the two and no binoculars or telescope to hand, I could only guess that what I saw that so inspired me was the mountain that carried the park's name. I walked up to the wood lot where the best views to the west were, and tracked back and forth in front of the little wood lot trees scrutinizing the forested mountains, trying to gain a sense of the multiple layering of ridges, the relative heights and distances. I was a little girl again, with her eyes agog, puzzling, calculating, and staring for long periods at maps and mountains.

The family humoured me without much interest of their own. For weeks after I'd bought those maps, whenever I travelled in the area by car, I pointed at emerging glimpses of mountains and ridges, explaining to a switched-off audience my new-found knowledge. On one occasion I cried, 'Look, Look! There's Mount Dumpling, see, and Murrabrine Mountain. It's six hundred and fifty metres high, you know, or thereabouts – the map is not all that clear. Someone should draw much better maps. Did you know...'

'Mum,' Sarah said in response. 'You're crazy.'

No, I'm not, I'm sane. It's the man-made world that's gone mad.

A few weeks later, sitting in the passenger seat of my little red car, I had another map in my hands. This time it was a mud map with Gino's wife Patto's directions. Greg liked to drive, and as I had no confidence on dirt roads, I relaxed and enjoyed the scenery. We'd been to Patto and Gino's only once last year for Gino's fiftieth birthday party. It was my first Australian bush bash, replete with oil drum braziers, a stage for music in an open-fronted tee-pee with Damon performing, and scores of bearded bushies, tents, kids, dogs and tables full of delicious-looking food. It had been a year for fiftieth birthday parties. After Laura's, the day the deluge flooded our floor, we were also invited to my employers at the post office Peter and Sylvia's joint fiftieth at the School of Arts hall. Damon played that time too, and we danced to U2 and Talking Heads covers.

This time we were invited for a pizza firing to christen Gino's hand-built pizza oven.

We drove south to the next village, Quaama, where we turned west, heading inland towards the mountains. After a few kilometres of winding past dairy farms and small-holdings, the road turned to dirt and we entered the bush. Greg dropped back into fourth gear and then into third as the road, now a track, wended its way up a hill, more like a small mountain. Cresting the rise, we passed into another world, sweeping views of rolling-green farmland giving way to the dramatically enclosed feeling of native forest. The further inland we travelled, the higher and steeper the hills became. The native forest enshrouded us in its uniquely magical atmosphere, stringy barks and southern mahoganies towering above an under-story of wattles, pea bushes and vines.

Steep-sided valleys became narrow gorges, the tree-lined road, a long series of hairpin bends. With the mountains ahead of us we climbed another hill, hoping it was the last one. By now the hills were around five hundred metres, the height of Mount Dumpling. It seemed like the kind of place you wouldn't want your car to break down in, and yet in every valley along the track, land had been zoned for small-holdings, and a smattering of caravans, sheds and houses appeared through the trees. The rugged hinterland of Wadbilliga remained devoid of human activity. It was home to wallabies, possums, parrots, wombats and snakes.

One more hill and a dozen hairpins and I spotted their driveway. We had arrived, almost. The driveway had deep ruts, pot holes and large bumps, and a gradient that made me wonder if we'd topple backwards. Stopping would not be an option. I closed my eyes as Greg made a run for it.

We parked under a tall stringy bark and Gino appeared. His warm eyes looked down at us with a smile.

'Thanks for coming.'

'Thanks for inviting us,' I said, 'I feel privileged to be here.'

It sounded corny but it was exactly how I felt. I was in admiration of the spirit it took to live so remotely. Patto and Gino were living a similar dream to us. They were frontier people. Physically tough with marshmallow hearts, their love of the land and an equal love of the fringes had drawn them to the edge of civilisation. Their property was almost at the end of the track. They needed a generator for electricity and had no phone connection to date. Beyond their property there was a patch of flat grazing land nestled in another steep-sided valley near the head of the Brogo dam. I'd seen it on the map. Beyond that was the wilderness.

A forest of stringy barks, mahoganies and red gums were interspersed with casuarinas and black wattle. I was enveloped in the invigorating scent of eucalyptus. Gino and Patto had a secluded, secret place, a little too rugged and wild for comfort, and yet the bush felt at once magical, benevolent and nurturing. In contrast to Voltaire's Garden, there was no horizon. Panoramas were replaced with close-ups. I found myself adjusting the way I viewed the scenery to appreciate what lay immediately in front of me.

I loved it, and part of me dreamed of it, but I knew I could never live in the bush surrounded by towering trees, precipitous gullies and vast granite faces just a kilometre or two from an area rarely entered by humans. There were no tracks through the Brogo wilderness, at least I couldn't find any marked on the topographical maps. To be so close to nature you had to be at ease with the emptiness, the isolation, the constant not-knowing what was out there and, not least, you had to be at ease with critters. I could live, nervously, with spider wasps, red back spiders and deadly funnel webs; even the red-bellied black snakes didn't bother me as long as there was a decent distance between us, but I needed a safe place run to, a solid house sealed off from the great outdoors.

Patto was different. In Patto I sensed another Agnes with a touch of my old neighbour Jo. When Patto emerged between the trees, it was as if she had come straight out of one of my enduring fantasies and walked into my life. She was a quintessential earth mother, with her long wavy hair framing an open, friendly face, her kind eyes and welcoming smile made me melt. I could have snuggled in the folds of her long frock, eaten her food, drank her wine and rested in her bosom forever. It was lovely to feel so close to someone without knowing them well, like the warmth and security of a protective mother, like I'd felt with Agnes.

Gino had lit the pizza oven early that morning. They'd brought across from their kitchen, located on another saddle, an esky with pizza toppings and another with beer. Planks of wood laid out on pallets of cement served as a kitchen table. Huge poles supporting an iron roof were in-filled with compressed straw panels – recycled sound proofing from a university building. Patto called the space the Cantina, in homage to the amount of large scale catering she'd undertaken here for numerous family gatherings.

Soon I saw a dark-haired man walking towards us. It was their neighbour Anthony, a keen gardener and prolific propagator whose seedlings Patto had passed on to us one time. I was delighted to tell him face to face how well his tomato and capsicums grew in our garden, and how grateful we were for his grape vines and pumpkin seeds.

Another couple arrived from a nearby property, and beer and wine began to flow, and human voices eclipsed the chattering, twittering, croaking sounds of the bush.

'Come on guys, let's make pizza,' Patto said, beckoning us to the table, now strewn with bowls of sliced vegetables, grated cheese and a plethora of sauces.

While the other guests joined in pizza assembly and Gino tended the fire, I settled into a chair facing the pizza oven, feeling exhausted with leaden arms, regretting my decision to paint the walls and ceiling of one of the guest rooms earlier that day. Pine-lining boards were impossible to paint with a roller, so I'd used what we had: a three-inch paint brush.

Gino's oven worked perfectly, producing pizza after pizza, each one oozing topping. Anthony and Greg chatted about gardening, and I tried desperately to maintain a conversation with the other guests. Still seated in the same chair, I looked up into their friendly happy faces, wondering for how long I could maintain a convivial, engaged demeanour when I was so exhausted.

The evening shadows lengthened and, holding a glass of wine that never seemed empty, I began to slump further into the chair. When Patto invited us to retire to their campsite on the next hill, I was barely able to stand up. Anthony took the opportunity to walk home. The other guests helped Patto clear the Cantina and drove her back to their home base. Realising our car wouldn't make the drive, Gino offered us a ride in his old Holden Kingswood ute. It was almost dark as he picked his way, ultra-slow, down a breathtaking descent, across a water course, and up an equally steep ascent on the other side, crossing one of Puen Buen's ubiquitous steep-sided gullies. We came to a halt on a small saddle of the next hill.

After easing myself unsteadily out of the ute, I stood facing north-east, where the valley below opened onto an undulating plain enclosed by forested hills. A full moon rose between the branches of a dead tree, bathing the landscape in its cool, silvery light. I heard my name and pulled myself away.

Behind me on the saddle, Patto and Gino had created an open-air living space plucked straight from one of my own fantasies. To my left, a cobbled together row of caravans, lean-tos and sheds flanked the saddle's eastern slope, ahead a huge shade house covered in bird-netting protected vegetables and fruit trees, and between the shade house and the caravans, there were little garden beds edged with bush rock and paths to connect each structure to the next. It was pixie heaven.

Inside, we sat in a makeshift living room, with corrugated iron and recycled timber walls, its rammed earth floor covered in lovely old rugs. It felt homely, replete with soft furnishings, cushions, shelving, a TV and a reasonably functioning kitchen at one end.

Patto poured more wine into my never-empty glass and I felt too tired to stop her. Then Gino told us his latest story.

He'd been heading to Sydney and had just passed Wollongong in his old Holden Kingswood when a police car appeared behind him. He knew the police would be doing a check on his vehicle. You don't see many Holden Kingswood utes like his on the road. Sitting in his jalopy looking like an old hippy from the bush, he was convinced he'd get stopped for a vehicle check, but the police car just kept following him. Worried that the speedo wasn't working, he slowed down. The police car stayed on his tail. Now he was sure they'd stop him. But they didn't. Instead, they passed by slowly, the cop in the passenger seat grinning at him. As they pulled in front, Gino saw the sign in their rear window, the one that usually told the driver to pull over. It was flashing, Overtaking Tortoise... Overtaking Tortoise...

'What a bloody cheek,' Gino said, 'I wasn't going that slow.'

The room filled with laughter. He left the room and returned with a torch.

'Let's go to the living room,' he said. 'I've lit a fire.'

Isn't this it? I thought, but staggered to my feet anyway, not wanting to be left behind.

We followed the pixie path past the shade house to a large lean-to, closed in on two sides and furnished with huge comfy sofas, cushions and rugs. A stereo was playing some recent Tom Jones. The others chatted gaily and chortled occasionally at a joke, but I couldn't maintain my upright position a moment longer. The last sip of wine had made my head swim. Seeing me slump, Patto laid me on the sofa and covered me with a large blanket. With eyes closed, Tom Jones in my ears and an image of Patto's nurturing ways in my head, I was utterly content to lie, listen, and be for a while.

A few minutes later, I was not so sure I wanted to be there.

Something had wriggled under the blanket. I could feel it jiggle and twitch on my calf through my jeans. I tried to ignore it, but it did it again, this time, halfway up my right thigh. Shaken into hyper-alertness, I leaped to my feet, patting myself down.

'Something is in that blanket!' I yelled, trembling.

'Oh, come on Isobel, there's nothing there,' Patto said with a laugh, shaking out the blanket and lifting sofa cushions. 'There's nothing. You've got the DT's.'

Maybe she was right. Now that I was standing I felt woozy again so I lay back down and drew up the blanket. Within thirty seconds there it was again. This time it had wriggled inside my jeans and was slinking its way up the back of my right trouser leg. It felt cool and slightly damp. Like a baby snake.

I was instantly on my feet.

'Bloody hell, there's something down my pants!'

My heart was pounding like a kettle drum. With my left hand I grasped at the writhing reptilian lump through my trouser leg to stop it travelling any higher, and I thrust my right hand down inside the back of my jeans and hauled the thing out. It plopped on the floor some way off. Patto grabbed a torch and a stick to flick it further off. She said it was dead. I'd killed it.

'What was it?'

Everyone wanted to know.

'Just a critter,' Patto said.

A critter! What kind of critter? One that bites, one that stings, one that can kill you, or what? I had no idea, Patto wouldn't tell me. I tried to convince myself it was only a skink.

My heart was still racing and I was no longer woozy and tired. Even with the soporific effects of the alcohol it took many minutes to calm down. After my ordeal, I sat on a hard-backed chair until it was time to go home.

Gino had no intention of driving us back to our car. He walked us to the Holden, showed Greg the gears and warned him of the quirks, and left us to make our way back through the steep-sided gully.

Gino had made it look easy. Peering over the steering wheel, Greg stayed in first gear as he directed the Holden over the uneven, bulbous track. We bounced our way down the precipitous hill, and bounced our way up the other side, two small people in the Holden's cavernous cabin, caroming and cackling like teenagers at a theme park, my squeals and shrieks and the Holden's rumbling engine as raucous as the hullabaloo of the bush.

After the pizza firing, I decided to be more pro-active about socialising. I needed people and a community, and I was surrounded by so many lovely friends who I rarely saw. It was time to reach out, connect, start feel I belonged here; I'd spent too long missing Ghana and my English friends, too long missing Agnes and Jo. If I didn't free myself from the internal prison I'd created, penned in by bars of bitterness and grief, I would forego new friendships, new experiences, and wither like a weed growing lonely in a crack in the concrete. I had longed to visit Wadbilliga, and I hadn't seen Dave and his partner Debra for months. I gave Debra a call and invited them for a picnic beside the Wadbilliga River.

At home a few days later, I was once again staring out the dining-room windows at Wadbilliga. It was a glorious day, the sun shone and the October air was still.

My reverie was interrupted by the telephone. It was Debra. She'd phoned with news that their daughter Ruby was unwell.

'But don't cancel. Dave is really keen to go.'

'Are you sure?' I said, disappointed, 'Why don't we arrange a different day?'

'I'd seize the opportunity. Dave's really busy. You go and enjoy yourself and we'll catch up soon.'

Shortly before ten Dave pulled up beside the garage in Landcare's Nissan Patrol. Greg was weeding the abelias along the front path. Five minutes later I saw them chatting by the hakeas in the infirmary.

I opened the front door and called out to them. 'Come in for a coffee.'

Inside, we spread a map over the dining table and I traced my fingers over the fire trails and logging tracks.

'Have you been on any of these, Dave?'

'Not yet. But I've done Conway's Gap. This one here.' He pointed.

'Me too,' Greg said. 'It's a great view up there.'

'We're only going here though,' I said, pointing to the picnic area, 'Shall I bring the map?'

'No need. There's one in the car.'

Greg filled water bottles and I packed a few sandwiches and we had a coffee before we set off.

'In case I forget, do you guys want a pumpkin?'

'I'd never say no to that, Isobel.'

I fetched a large Queensland Blue and Dave uttered a soft, 'Wow,' as he took it.

Are we ready?'

He was as eager as me. His nine-to-five Landcare job involved more administration that he cared for. His preference was to be outdoors, caring for the land, not trapped in an office by paperwork.

On the front porch, I pulled on my new work boots. We were all set. I sat in the passenger seat next to Dave, a privileged position as organiser of the event. Greg climbed in the back with the pumpkin.

We followed the road twenty-three kilometres to Yowrie. Then Dave pointed to the land to our right and told us it used to be a hanging swamp. He said all through the area used to be natural springs and babbling brooks, but then White man came with his cattle and the whole lot got eroded. No more swamp, just creeks with eroded embankments.

Soon we entered the Wadbilliga National Park. The sealed road became dirt and we wended our way through hairpins and over a high hill, descending a few hundred metres before the road levelled off and we were following the Wadbilliga River, about a hundred metres below. The road continued to follow the river until we reached a camping area, the road now descending to meet the river at a ford. Across the ford I saw the picnic area in a clearing to the left, nestling in a sheltered spot underneath the canopy of a magnificent Manna gum, its luminescent trunk exposed through a cascade of bark shards.

After an early lunch Greg and Dave walked to the river bank, obscured from the picnic area by a screen of tall trees and bushy undergrowth, while I cleared away the picnic, collected my camera and followed. By the time I got to the bank they'd already crossed the river. I saw them admiring native vines growing in the fractured granite face sheltering the far bank. Giant pink-granite pebbles littered the riverbed. Crystal-clear water gurgled and splashed, and overhanging branches of huge Manna gums shaded the narrow bank on the other side.

Greg and Dave had picked their way across the pebbles to cross the river. I tried to follow but my stiff new boots made my steps feel slippery and precarious. I made it across, but they were now much further ahead. When I finally caught up, I found them exploring the flora close to the cliff where giant fig tree roots wending down cracks in the granite to the soil below, and huge, heavy vines, tree ferns and rock orchids were scattered about. It was exquisite here, silent but for the sounds of splashing water and birds.

When we returned to the car, I expected to go home, but Dave spread the map on the bonnet.

'Not much further and we'll be up at Conway's Gap,' he said. 'It's on the top of the escarpment. You should see it, Isobel. It's really is impressive. And there's something else I want to show you. Fancy exploring?'

I paused for a moment and peered at the map, but without my reading glasses the blue, orange and red lines were a blur. Dave could not only see the map, I knew he could read it, too.

'Sure,' I said at last.

Greg needed no encouragement. We piled back in the ute and followed the road past the picnic area, where it disappeared through the trees.

The road rose rapidly, twisting and winding round hairpin bends in an increasingly steep ascent, the fall on my side of the road becoming more and more dramatic as the gorge below narrowed. I eased my way towards Dave and looked straight ahead, preferring to admire the forest of tree ferns, hakeas, banksias, lilli pillis, soft grasses and huge manna gums overhanging the road than look down at what I knew was there – a precipitous drop into a deepening gorge, the cliff rising up the other side in a series of sheer granite faces. This was the Wadbilliga gorge.

We climbed to a thousand metres, reaching the top of the escarpment where the road turned sharply to the right. A sign to the left read Conway's Gap. Dave stopped the ute.

Dave and Greg were already at the edge staring at the facing cliffs when I alighted gingerly, easing my way around the ute, then pressing my back to the embankment on the other side of the track. My palms were sweaty, my breath short. I was petrified, but desperately wanted to look. When Dave and Greg stood closer towards the edge, pointing at this and that, I trembled in terror. My knees weakened and I felt faint.

'Let's go on a bit further,' Dave said as they made their way back to the ute. 'The vegetation changes dramatically up here.'

I slid my way around the back and side of the ute, and got in.

I said nothing. They said nothing. It was clear to me though that Dave was ignoring my fear. Greg was also ignoring my fear. No words of comfort, just bland indifference. I supposed they thought I'd get over it or I was play acting.

Round another bend the land plateaued and we were surrounded by a heathland of dwarf casuarinas and grevillias and banksias, punctuated by stands of scrubby mallee eucalypts. The casuarinas were in flower, covering the heath in a rust-red mantle.

Dave pulled over again. We all decanted and he spread the map on the bonnet. It was beginning to dawn on me that he had his own agenda for the day, one that meant he would not be heading back to the office.

'If we can get through here,' he said, pointing to a track that cut across the Tuross River, through some farms, and back across the Tuross to the escarpment, 'we can reach the razorback fire trail.'

'The razorback?' I said, suddenly enthusiastic.

The razorback fire trail was the last track before the wilderness and when I'd studied it on the map at home, I saw that it followed a ridgeline. The trail led to Wadbillaga Mountain, the locus of my obsession with the terrain. Overlooking my manifest fear of heights, I wondered if from the mountain I would be able to look down on Cobargo and even our house.

'Let's do it!'

Dave folded up the map. Greg was silent. He was like a boy scout having a grand adventure, a three-year-old with matchboxes of stinky barnacles, occupied this time filling his pockets with seeds.

We followed the road across the Tuross River – little more than a stream – passing heath, pasture and alpine forest before gaining access through unlocked gates, and then carrying on by run-down dwellings, outbuildings and a caravan, all empty. Then we headed back across the Tuross, through more heath and onto the razorback fire trail. The grey kangaroos and rock wallabies grazing nearby hopped away, startled.

At first, the trail was smooth and the terrain quite flat as we were still on the plateau. It was not long, though, before we reached the escarpment. At this point, the mountains extruded towards the coast in a profusion of ridges, gullies and gorges. We followed the trail as the land to each side of us narrowed and before much longer we were traversing an undulating ridge. The trail itself gradually deteriorated, becoming boulder-strewn, and fit only for four-wheel drive vehicles. Dave kept his hands on the steering wheel at a reassuring ten-to-two. He had no choice. He also had no choice but to keep going. The trail was not wide enough for a U-turn. Greg, behind me on the back seat, chatted to Dave about native flora. I stopped listening. I focused entirely on reminding myself that Dave was a competent driver and nothing untoward was likely to happen. We were not, absolutely not about to topple down the steep escarpment to either side of us. No, no, that simply wasn't possible. Was it?

Just as I began to feel at ease with the trail's condition and Dave's driving, the land to either side of us fell away dramatically, leaving an isthmus of about five metres wide. I glanced through my side window, taking in the steep, forested slope plummeting down to the valley some thousand metres below. The only security was afforded by a thin screen of trees miraculously rooted to the mountainside. When I looked across the valley at the mountains on the other side of the deep valley my head began to swim, my heart pumped hard in my chest and palms broke out in sweat. I couldn't watch for long, just a glance, barely enough to absorb the scene, but long enough to know it. Granite bluffs crowned the mountainous ridges, and beneath them the land swept down to the valley floor in voluminous undulations of saddle and gully, a vast ocean swell of green forest in a giant water-catchment basin. In the valley floor, Wadbilliga River flowed through a narrow, granite gorge, straight at first, before arcing out of view beyond the mountains.

I looked at my feet to help me calm down.

Ignoring my terror or oblivious to it, Dave kept driving, now at less than walking speed. Then, inexplicably, he stopped.

Looking up, I found we were still on the isthmus. I glanced right this time, at another, even vaster basin. It was as steep, as deep, and as dramatic as the basin on my side, its undulating, green, forest, kilometres wide. That basin contained the headwaters of Brogo River, feeding the Brogo dam downstream.

One glimpse and my eyes were again focussed on the floor.

Then Dave unbuckled his seatbelt and Greg opened his door and I could contain my panic no longer. Sure, all that scenery was magnificent to behold. Sure, it was one of those once-in-a-lifetime views you just had to stop and savour. And no doubt there was no wind to suddenly sweep us off the edge. And none of us was about to plummet to a certain death. But there was no rationalising away my terror. With my eyes firmly locked in a grim stare at my feet, I said between gritted teeth, 'Why the hell stop here.'

I must have sounded as hysterical as I felt. Without a word,

Greg closed his door and Dave secured his seatbelt. We were moving again at walking speed.

I kept looking down at my feet. My imagination had absorbed the landscape like Polaroid in a camera with a fast shutter speed. My feelings of awe, wonder, reverence and fear were gained firsthand through several visual flashes, and then second-hand, through imaginative reconstructions. Even when staring at my feet, too petrified to raise my head, my peripheral vision remained, luring my eyes towards the windows, tempting me to battle fear and snatch another glance, wanting, yearning to embrace the panorama's glorious presence and gain a sense of truth of the natural world. Fear of the abyss was in a titanic struggle with my strong desire to be at one with the world now in front of me, to immerse myself in its consummate beauty for a while. Fear won.

When we had at last driven across the isthmus, Dave stopped the car once more. Now we were on a plateau and there was no view to behold. He spread the map on the bonnet and traced his finger along the trail.

'This is Wadbilliga Mountain, right here,' he said, pointing. 'There's a trig point somewhere up there,' he indicated to the north. 'Trig points are used in orienteering.'

I hung back while they scrutinized the map, deciding whether to continue or turn back. Then I left them and wandered in the direction of the invisible trig point, convinced I would find a walking track to the summit. The land was almost flat. Large granite standing stones interspersed with a thin forest of snowy gums and heath leant the terrain an eerie, inhospitable atmosphere. I walked a little further. Then I heard Dave calling me back. When I turned, he was pointing at a large, male, grey kangaroo looking our way. I had no sense of fear and couldn't understand what he meant. Then Greg waved me back too. He seemed urgent. Deflated, I returned to the car. It wasn't until I had reached the ute and was told of the dangers male kangaroos posed when threatened, that I realised my fear instinct was remarkably unreliable.

They were still discussing the trail. Dave looked at his watch. It was two o'clock. We'd traversed five kilometres of the trail so far, and had another eleven to go before we were off the razorback, and then a further seven kilometres before we would exit Wadbilliga at Puen Buen.

Dave studied the map again, looking for visual guides, natural signposts that would lead us in the right direction, tracing his finger further along the trail.

'These are switchbacks.'

'Switchbacks?' I said.

I squinted at the map. Dave indicated a patch of tightly packed contour lines with squiggly red dashes marked down them. I'd never heard of a switchback and didn't ask for an explanation.

'After the switchbacks we can take the Brandy Creek trail. We should be able to leave the park at the head of the Brogo dam, if the gates are not locked.'

He sounded optimistic. He seemed to know what he was talking about. We continued.

The condition of the trail worsened, the boulders becoming larger and larger as we followed the precipitous undulations of the ridge. Dave called the ridge bony, a reference to the razorback – a wild, narrow-bodied pig with a ridged back. I had no clear idea why I hadn't cottoned on to the significance of the name until that moment. The name was apt, only the scale differed, and we were not coursing the spine of a pig, rather it felt like we were traversing the spine of a colossal dinosaur. It was a roller coaster ride in slow motion, tortuously steep rises, declivitous descents, each one more terrifying than the last.

After descending into another dip with the land to either

side falling away, Dave again stopped the car. Ahead we faced the next rise, the steepest and highest so far.

'What do you think?' he said to Greg on the back seat.

'I've seen worse, I think.'

'What else can we do?' I said.

'We can't turn back.'

'You're right,' Greg said peering down at the road. 'Doesn't look like the road is wide enough here to turn the car around.'

'Okay. Here goes.'

I was silent. I felt weak.

Dave continued in low, low range, traveling at a slow walk. The car followed what looked like a vertical ascent, even steeper when we had to mount the deep swales constructed to prevent erosion.

Now panic was causing me to babble. I began to exclaim and laugh hysterically in a monotonous running commentary, as repetitive and irritating as a sports commentator at an uneventful football game.

Dave tried to reassure me of his driving experience and special training on a four-wheel driving course, but I could tell we were all becoming worried. We had no food, little water and, it transpired, no chain saw and no bolt cutters. Just a ruddy pumpkin rolling about on the backseat next to Greg.

We'd agreed to make our foray into the wilderness beyond the picnic site on impulse. If that gate at the end of the fire trail at Puen Buen was locked or a tree had fallen across the trail, we'd have to head back the way we'd come, if we could find a place to turn around. It was now three o'clock. In a few hours it would be dark.

The trees to either side of us were now rough grey iron and stringy barks, but their solid forms afforded scant security from the ever-present, precipitous drop.

It was when we reached the switchbacks that I realised

what a switchback was – a zigzag down a cliff. On sealed roads with crash barriers and reasonably wide bends driving through them was not difficult. But the switchbacks we approached were not like that. It was as if someone had gouged the granite face with an awl in sharp, angry lines, like an attempt to scribble over unwanted graffiti in a public toilet.

I had all but given up looking. I had never driven directly down a cliff face before and I didn't want to embrace the experience now. Some fifteen hundred metres high, we began the descent. Each turn was sharp, the first barely wide and deep enough to accommodate the length of Dave's ute. I could feel us losing traction as one of the back wheels threatened to slip over the edge.

My heart was doing somersaults. I was so frightened I felt myself leaving my body.

Meanwhile, Greg, fearless in the back, was incredulous that anyone could have constructed a trail here.

'Why bother?' he said. 'I can't see the point of it myself.'

'It's the only place they could get a fire trail through,' Dave said. 'Everywhere else is too rugged.'

I couldn't imagine anywhere more rugged than this. I caught a glimpse of Greg on the backseat winding down his window to peer down the cliff and I nearly shrieked.

Dave managed to navigate round each switchback driving at the pace of a snail.

Four kilometres of the same bony terrain and we left the Razorback only to find the Brandy Creek trail was no better. Even Dave was getting uneasy.

It was dusk when we reached the flatter terrain of Puen Buen and I began to relax, but not for long as finding our way out of the forest proved difficult in the gloaming, the trail petering out in a flat-bedded valley with smaller, disued tracks heading off in all directions. It was a desolate, eerie place, and we wanted to get out before nightfall. Signs of human habitation and activity rendered the scene more ominous still. On our many false attempts at an exit we passed an abandoned spot mill, its rusted, circular saw blade still in place, an iron lean-to housing rusty jerry cans, a hut more like a dog kennel and a dilapidated caravan. About half an hour passed before we managed to find the right track that led to a gate. We heard dogs barking in the distance and, as we neared the gate, we saw four huge padlocks hanging from it. I held my breath while Greg went to check on them, convinced we were about to have to turn around and repeat that entire terrifying trip in reverse in the dark.

To our relief, Greg found none of the locks were in use and he hurriedly opened the gate and waited for Dave to drive through, all the while looking around nervously for dogs.

As we passed through the gate I felt I was crossing a threshold, leaving a place of primordial splendour, a place terrifying, exhilarating and reverently beautiful, to enter the more sedate, human world, safe and secure. No doubt Greg felt the same once he'd closed the gate and got back into the ute as a snarly black beast of a canine headed our way.

A gibbous moon rose in the east lighting the journey home. I was still a little hysterical and babbled continuously for a while. At the same time, I was aware how powerfully affected I was on a much deeper level. Fear had brought me closer to humanity's primal urge to survive than on any previous occasion, and an appreciation of the glorious beauty I glimpsed on the razorback had instilled new hope, an optimism based upon my homage to a tantalisingly unknowable other embodied in the mountains.

I had no doubt that the wilderness could change people. It lifted us far beyond ordinary waking experience and touched something deep inside us. The wilderness was strange; it owed us nothing, was heedless and seemed to offer no sense of direction. It was a place of mystery and unknowing. In time and in stillness, experiencing the wilderness had the same transformative potential as a mystical experience. We might return unchanged, or we might absorb the experience into our being, reorient ourselves, choose a different direction in life. Those were my rational if euphoric thoughts floating around in my mind the following day.

The mountains of Wadbilliga had given me the greatest hope for humanity. They reflected the magnitude of the natural world, at once known and unknown, mysterious, secret and precious; mountains that demanded reverence and inspired awe. Silent, timeless and completely indifferent to us, mountains spoke of the enormous power of the earth. Before a mountain, whether at its base or on its summit, we stood like ants – tiny, in right proportion with the natural world, humbled and insignificant. The meaning and purpose of our existence lies there, in relation to the mountains; their breadth, height and ineffable depth symbolic of aeons. They were for us real and immutable, not an abstraction, an ideal existing only in our minds.

CHAPTER SIX

WORK AND COMMUNITY

'I also know,' said Candide, 'that we must go and work in the garden.'

G ardening had become the centre of my working life; work well worth doing because the rewards were enormous. Gardens were fun. I thought of a garden as a canvas, a template for decades of creative expression. All gardens involved work, but it was pleasurable, outdoors work, even when arduous.

After nearly eighteen months of toil, our garden had taken shape. Trees had grown, some astoundingly fast, while others had borne fruit. Herbs had spread to form carpets of purple and gold. One tree planted in the paddock had become the centre-piece of a large garden bed. And a hillside covered in paddock grasses was now a series of terraces descending to the dam. The old red gums in the gully to the northeast rose above the garden trees in an enveloping arc, providing mottled shade and a habitat for countless birds, many of whom had taken up residence to enjoy the newly emerging habitat. Greg had created moist zones and well-drained zones to support various kinds of plants through his attention to water harvesting and management of water flows. I had planted strategically to take account of the arc of the sun and direction of the prevailing winds, so that every tree and shrub, every vegetable and herb had a suitable location. I was impressed by the diversity of food stuffs already in the ground, amazed at how a few acres of garden could support so much variety: Sun loving almonds and dry-loving grapes, cool loving apples and raspberries, figs, avocadoes, pecans, olives, citrus, plums, peaches and apricots, and every kind of vegetable.

Towards the end of last summer bumper crops meant a day's pick brought into the kitchen each day buckets full of ripe Roma tomatoes, cucumbers by the dozen, kilos of beans, scores of zucchinis and at least five capsicums. A chaotic mix of shiny, bright reds, oranges and greens strewn over the benches became a creative delight of pickling and chutney making. And then there was the basil, which I would harvest all through summer and autumn until the leaves shrivelled and rotted in the cool nights of May. The more I picked, the bushier the basil became, until the basil beds formed a metre-high mass laden with leaves.

There was only one way to use large quantities of basil – make pesto. In summer we ate pesto for dinner every second or third night, and although we loved it we could never consume enough to keep abreast of the superb growth, and since basil was one of those herbs that oxidises quickly and does not dry or freeze well, I tended to give my surplus away. Otherwise I'd need to compost the tips I pruned, which seemed a terrible waste, almost a crime.

To begin with in basil season whenever someone visited I

invited them to pick some. It began with our neighbours John and Hillary, when we were living in the annex last year. Shortly after their visit, Patto and Gino dropped by with an offer of free bantam chickens, and left with two bags of basil. The following weekend, when Peter arrived to collect his daughter Vanessa he, too, left with a bag full. He was ecstatic, his southern Italian blood warming at the thought of fresh pesto, his fingers itching for more time in his own garden. In return, he gave us some macadamia nuts from his tree. I had given bags of basil to Acko, our plasterer Mal, and even a driver delivering hardware. I asked Charlie too, but he had plenty of his own.

These occasional visits were not enough to reduce the enormous basil crop. I began to phone friends. Out of all those who helped with the glut, it was Debra and her daughter Ruby who saved the basil from going to seed. Ruby, then five, loved to mingle among basil bushes, almost as tall as she, to pick the tips. On warm late-summer afternoons, I would bunch my dress between my thighs, hand Debra a bag and we picked and picked until our bags were full. Debra adored our place. Maybe it represented one of her unlived lives.

One day she asked if it was okay to pass the basil on to others.

'Absolutely!' I said, looking at three bags full of basil tips and two beds still laden with leaves. Basil had become my symbol for giving and the simple, natural, joyous feeling that came with it, as uplifting as the basil was aromatic. If I were to believe that ambition could be considered a virtue, it would have to be an ambition to give abundantly, and the selfish satisfaction felt when the receiver smiles in gratitude.

On one of Deb's visits she arrived with a small envelope in her hand. It was a wedding invitation. She and Dave had decided to get married. It was to be a large gathering of family and friends held outdoors in a beautiful clearing along the Bermagui River, the home of close friends and founders of The Crossing, whose fundraiser four years earlier was where I met Greg.

On the day of their wedding, we packed up early and I prepared a plate of tomatoes on a bed of basil and salad greens for the wedding feast, while Greg organised our gift. Dave and Debra asked their guests to bring some kind of material that could be incorporated into a large weaving. Dave suggested people brought lengths of coloured wool, feathers, or strands of leather. Greg had another idea. He split a long piece of electrical wire into its three strands and plaited them together. As part of the ceremony each guest was invited to write the special meaning or significance of their offering in the wedding book. In the wedding book Greg wrote:

Greg, Isobel, Mary and Sarah wish you an electrifying life together – stare deeply into the plastic and you will see...an ancient cycad forest or a long dead tree...no sense of dislocation between man-made and what occurs naturally...we are one as you in your union become one...go forward famously

We arrived late and followed the sound of drumbeats down to a green field in a sheltered valley. The ceremony had begun. People gathered around a stage. We stood amongst pavilions, flags and pennons, mingling with a host of gaily dressed and happy people. Behind us a string quartet were tuning their instruments. Under a large marquee a sumptuous feast was laid. Beside it, on the floor, eskies filled with champagne and ice waited.

The ceremony touched our hearts. Debra and Dave stood

proud and joyous on a small dais with their children, Ruby and
A J.

Resplendent in a burnt orange dress, Debra was the perfect
companion for Dave. She had the softest brown eyes and her
hair was dark, wavy and flowing, and she exuded the same
warmth from within. She was a beautiful woman, a former
model, and her natural elegance matched Dave's earthy
composure.

We listened as they enacted their scripted ceremony.
Children fidgeted and played, and couples of all ages began to
edge closer to each other as the ceremony progressed, some
holding hands, others wrapping their arms around each other.
Greg sidled closer, his arm reaching round my waist.

I suddenly found myself fighting back tears, overwhelmed
by the feeling of community, the warmth, the joyous union of
two dear friends, and an equally powerful sense of loss and
sadness, an absence, of all the people in my life I had loved and
farewelled never to encounter again, and of all the places I had
lived and never re-visited. It was Polesworth and Pampawie
again, making my heart ache, two short weeks in Ghana that I
had often felt should have been a lifetime. Another life, only
partially lived, a treasured dream of making a difference in a
suffering world.

How different their wedding was from ours. Standing
beside Greg watching the wedding couple kiss, I could sense
the romance and the blessings from the gathering of family and
friends. Cast in that light, our wedding seemed more a
pragmatic event. Even the proposal lacked the romance
normally associated with marriage.

The idea had occurred to me lying in bed one late winter's
morning.

'Why don't we get married?' I said.

'Okay.'

As simple as that.

We were ambivalent at first about a conventional wedding, but after much discussion we decided to marry in Carolyn's Presbyterian church. It was my idea, to please his mother. The reception was held at my sister Michele's house which was large enough to accommodate the thirty guests we invited. Greg asked Damon to be best man and chauffeur and wedding entertainer. Sarah and Mary were bridesmaids and Michele matron of honour. I bought the rings and my mother made the wedding cake. Greg and I doubled as caterers, and it was lucky we had a bountiful autumn harvest.

On the day, I arrived at the Church wearing a wedding dress I found for fifteen dollars in Vinnies, a charity shop in Narooma. Greg and Damon were already at the altar. Greg looked dashing in a twenty-dollar, pure wool suit, also from Vinnies.

I walked up the aisle on the arm of Bryan, when a sudden wave of almost uncontrollable panic made my legs wobble and my palms sweat. By the time I reached Greg, I was frozen in terror. I swallowed my voice as I spoke the vows and grinned stupidly through the whole ceremony. Greg, on the other hand, sailed through it all like the main character in a stage play.

I was so overcome with nerves I made a fast exit after the ceremony, and after politely greeting the smiling faces outside the Church, I bolted for Damon's car. Greg joined me after seemingly endless repartees, and it wasn't until Damon drove away, that I began to relax, gazing out the car window at the turquoise waters of the Wagonga inlet shimmering under the pale blue of a clear autumnal sky. The inlet was fringed by forested hills. Beyond, the pristine coastline coursed its way north, past rocky outcrops, and small bays of white sand. A light swell made the sapphire ocean waters heave in slow motion, my own heartbeat at last settling en rapport.

We wended our way through spotted gum forest until we entered a landscape of pastures dotted with small dams, devoted mostly to dairy cattle. When we reached the last hill before the descent into Cobargo and the trees were close to the road again, I leaned forward in my seat, knowing that ahead the landscape would open into a sweeping panorama. The moment was always dramatic, the world and the sky seemed to greet me in a welcoming, wide-armed embrace, as if a curtain was raised, revealing a scene from another time and another place.

What a contrast to Dave and Debra's wedding, which ended with the sound of African drumming, the music drawing the gathering away from the stage. There seemed not one moment of sadness or panic. Wine flowed without end. I felt relaxed, as mellow as the autumn sunset.

Now that the winter had passed, the days longer and the evening warmer, I felt a growing need for Voltaire's Garden to integrate with the local community. I started to feel guilty at not joining one of the numerous committees in the village, at not being pro-active. Greg was still focusing on the gardening and building tasks immediately ahead, and had little interest in socialising and I, too, was very busy, dashing back and forth to the literary agency in Bermagui, between hours of hard physical work at home. Sometimes I thought I must have been born with a gardening trowel in one hand and a paint brush in the other and a pen between my teeth.

For social contact, as ever we relied mostly on people dropping by and sometimes these visits were little chinks that illuminated our future plans for the place – bartering, borrowing, helping and swapping ideas, seeds, produce and skills.

We were always delighted to see a car travel up our driveway.

One day, from the living-room window I saw a white van pull up beside our garage and wondered who it could be.

I opened the front door to see Anthony, who we met at Patto and Gino's pizza firing, arrive with a small box of plants. Greg appeared from around the side of the house, having also seen the van arrive.

We walked Anthony around the garden as he told us how his Italian parents imbued him with a love of home-grown food and a real appreciation for taste. He said he knew many ways to train a grape vine and how to make mud bricks as he collected some seed from our dahlias and lamb's ears. He told us the best passionfruit vines were self-seeding opportunists that had passed through the gut of a bird.

I embraced Anthony's visit with passion, realising too, that there were many people residing in this region who aspired to the same values of fresh food and great flavours and a strong desire to provide what they could for themselves. Projects like ours abounded in this predominantly dairy farming region, each with their own particular specialty, whether it be a B&B or a cottage industry like honey, lavender, mustard, free range eggs, organic chickens, olives for oil, stone fruits or apples, berries and even farming snails, someone seemed to be doing it.

Perhaps Epicurus was right, living simply and not craving more and more, *was* satisfying and rewarding. It was a simple life and managed well, we would always have full bellies.

Later, standing by the dam under the old red gum with Greg, I looked to the west, past the adjoining paddocks and tree-lined creeks, beyond the undulating hills chequered lightly with trees and the occasional farmhouse to the mountains. The sky was clear, the sun bright, the horizon distinct. My eyes scanned the skyline of Wadbilliga and I felt, once again, a mysterious pull, as if a special secret was held within those magnificent mountain folds. Whatever the secret, it was the mountains that drew a certain type of person to this area and bound them in a perpetual state of wonder, enchantment and a determination to care for the environment, as if the mountains contained a concentration of nature's will that impelled us to care.

October was a busy month in the garden, by now the soil warm enough to plant out the first round of summer vegetables – green beans, zucchinis, capsicums, beetroot and tomatoes – leaving cucumbers and basil until early November, well past the chance of a late frost. For the first few weeks of the season, I protected the seedlings from cold winds and nights using cut-down plastic milk cartons.

Some vegetables I didn't need to bother with. Lettuces, for example, were already self-seeding like weeds, and pumpkins seemed to pop up everywhere, especially in the olive grove, thanks to Greg, his hoe, and the random burial of kitchen waste, undertaken largely pending our chicken coop and a much larger worm farm.

It was also his idea to purchase a diesel-powered rotary hoe, the preferred tool of the small-scale market gardener, and a large step up from the ox and plough. Our Valpadana was a self-propelled, walk-behind, rotary hoe. Also known as an Italian tractor, it was made in 1980 and we were told the company still made spare parts. Greg was impressed with the simplicity of its single-cylinder, crank-start diesel engine, its chunky solidity and the way its weight was perfectly poised at a point of balance over the axle.

Val' was our symbol of scale, spatially and technologically. Greg didn't want a ride-on lawn mower or a large tractor, and I was glad we did most things the manual labour way. We could have brought in machines long ago. We could have hired a trench digger to dig our trenches, or a back hoe to move dirt, dig the dish drain and level the terraces, but as Gino often said, it's easier to fix a mistake made with a spade than one made by a bulldozer. By using large machines, we would have avoided hours and hours of hard labour, but we would have traded the intimacy of getting to know the views and the wild life for a few hours of watching a noisy, fume-belching machine from a window. We would then not have noticed the bogongs mating on a little tree trunk, the fire spitting caterpillars decimating a spotted gum, weeds choking a baby tree, or any of the other little details that bring a person closer to the place they live. To enhance what was already there, in the contours of the land, the directions of the wind, the flow of the water, and the arc of the sun, we worked the land gently and slowly.

With Valpadana we could till the soil in preparation for sowing crops such as corn, potatoes, beans and chickpeas, and green manure – clovers, lucerne and farm peas – to fertilise the olive and almond groves. Our chickens, when we got them, would not only provide eggs and meat, they would eat kitchen scraps and provide fertiliser. Grazing lambs for slaughter was a passive way of mowing as well as food for the table. As for a milking cow, a nice idea now I knew how to make my own yogurt, butter and cheese, but I didn't fancy the twice daily milking. But I did want to make soap one day. My cleaning products cupboard contained white vinegar, bicarbonate of soda, washing soda and eucalyptus oil, all that after a lifetime of petro-chemical products.

Yet for all our back-to-earthing, it had to be said that Greg's small frame battling to hold onto and steer the rotary hoe as he flattened the rips housing the olive grove was hard to watch. He managed to avoid damaging the trees but at what cost to his arms and wrists and back.

Perhaps Greg and I had entered into a primal current in the human psyche, one cognizant and responsive to the basic needs of food, water and shelter. Sometimes we made mistakes, other times we had happy accidents. In our first year, Greg sowed a large bed of carrots and before I could use them many went to seed. I overlooked saving the seed partly because I'd heard that over a few generations, carrot seed reverts to something pale, thin and unappetizing, but mostly because I also read that pest-eating insects benefited from having clusters of tall leafy plants to hide in. So, I left them. Wind blew the seed across the terraces, most germinating in the herb garden on the top terrace, eventually creating a mass of feathery foliage that now swamped the thyme and rosemary bushes, and the asparagus, the liquorice root and the chives.

I stared at my carrot infestation one afternoon feeling a little overwhelmed by the prospect of dealing with so many carrots, but there was nothing to do other than start yanking them out. By the time I'd harvested three quarters of the patch, Peter and Laura's daughters Vanessa and Sarah stopped by to visit Mary. They hailed a hello and before they could turn their backs I rose to my feet and beckoned them over to where buckets and buckets of harvested carrots sat needing a wash.

'So many carrots,' Vanessa said.

'If you wouldn't mind, while you chat to Mary, would you scrub them clean for me?'

'Of course.'

Such obliging girls.

I organised more buckets and bowls, along with three

scrubbing brushes and set them up a work station at the edge of the courtyard. Emboldened, I returned to the terraces and pulled up the rest of the carrots like crazy. I pulled king and queen carrots over a foot long, standard soldiers erect and full of promise, and many contorted, gnarly nuggets. Large and small, Vanessa, Sarah and Mary scrubbed them all. It was lovely to watch them at work, their heads close together, two brunettes bookending Mary's red mane. Seeing them work so diligently brought home the undeniable fact that in moving to Cobargo, I had gifted my daughters innocence and the wholesome values of country living.

When they'd finished I found we'd harvested over twenty kilos and had a lovely, social time.

To celebrate, I made carrot juice.

It was a time of carrot soup, carrot salad, baked carrots and honeyed carrots. We still had pumpkins from last winter too, along with plenty of turnips and snow peas. I began to think we were about to drown in a sea of produce, but then I felt inspired to host a dinner party, the first in our new home. I invited Dave, Debra and Ruby, and Dave's mother Dawn and her partner Ivan, who'd recently moved to the village after selling their five acres of established food gardens in Candelo, seventy kilometres south.

I planned the menu around the harvest, leaving space in the first course for Deb's antipasto platter. With Ivan's bottles of home-made fruit wine, the scene was set for a good night's eating.

They arrived in a throng and I was surrounded by their warmth. As I hugged Debra, I nuzzled her long dark hair, smelling her scent, feeling the curve of her shoulders. She was a sensual woman who, like Greg, modelled for the life drawing class in the village. Dave's hug was strong; I felt I could melt into his arms. He gave forth a homely masculine feel, like pipes and slippers.

Ruby leaped into my arms before I could greet Dawn and Ivan, but over her shoulder I saw Greg steering them into the kitchen.

I loved the way that silent room became alive with chatter the moment guests arrived. A homey and intelligent woman, Dawn was immediately drawn to our vast collection of second-hand books, and noticed the Louis Bromfield.

'Ah, you've read him? What do you think of him?' she asked me.

'Not me. Greg.'

He was busy serving wine and she didn't distract him. We talked about the garden instead. Dawn had a keen interest in alternative ways of living, particularly those involving food. Her view coalesced with mine, and with her wide-ranging knowledge and experience, I found her informative. Before long she engaged Sarah then Mary, entertaining them with questions and stories from her life.

When seated we enjoyed Debra's platter and a large bowl of hummus I'd made earlier, served with wholemeal chapattis, which were so easy to make, I wondered why I didn't make them more often.

Greg and Ivan had developed an instant rapport, sitting together chatting until Greg cleared away plates. Then Ivan, looking impressive with his long white beard, talked us through wine-making and his methods for controlling fruit fly.

'We plan to erect a cage to enclose the whole orchard, but I guess bird wire won't keep the flies out,' I said.

'Shade cloth will keep the flies out,' said Mary.

She sat erect in her chair. I loved to see her doing that; I'd taught her not to develop a sway back when she was about six and she'd never forgotten.

'And keep the bees out too,' Greg said, 'and we want bees.'

'Can't you use fly spray?' was Sarah's remark. She was being playful, but Ivan was serious.

'It's best to use a range of methods. Dak pots for biological control, chickens to eat the larvae, and then of course you have to pick up all the fallen fruit.'

'Why bother?' Mary said.

'Because we like our fruit. It's healthy,' I said, rising to bring the next course.

I brought the vegetarian lasagna to the table. I'd made fresh pasta and used spinach, leeks and snow peas in a rich cheesy sauce as filling. I served it with roasted pumpkin topped with finely chopped rosemary and sea salt, honeyed carrots and beautifully creamy turnip puree laced with freshly ground nutmeg and black pepper.

It had seemed a good idea earlier in the day to roast pumpkin and prepare a large bowl of turnip puree to accompany the lasagne. Only now the dishes were placed together, I realised my mistake. My poor dinner guests faced an assemblage of steaming stodge. The colours were right, a good mix of red, orange and green, but the volume of carbohydrate was overwhelming, even to look at.

One by one we filled our plates, Dave and Ivan piling theirs high. Mouthful by mouthful the conversation slowed. Ruby slumped in her chair and began to look sleepy. So did Ivan. It was only his wine that was keeping the rest of us going.

'This is what life is all about, good food, good wine and good company!' Greg exclaimed with easy charm, raising his glass to inject some life back into the party.

'I agree,' Debra said, raising her glass.

We set down our glasses and continued to tackle our plates.

'How will you manage this place in ten years' time?' Ivan said.

Leaving his own five acres had been a wrench.

'Good question. When knees and backs wear out,' I said, with a nod to Mary and Sarah, my not-quite-so-willing free help. 'Greg's determined to make the place as easy to look after as possible.'

'The irony is that in the end the only way that projects like yours survive is by drawing on community support,' Dawn said.

'I think you're right. We started this thing with the idea of feeding ourselves from our own land and now people ask us if we are practicing permaculture or whether we are certified organic.'

'Not surprising. People assume that you would be.'

'Yes, but I am amazed at the way we have naturally adopted key aspects of a permaculture lifestyle.'

It was true, we read the land and the weather, we were owner building, we practiced land stewardship with our wood lot, we had a preference for organic food, and we were intent on seed saving and water management. We recycled and reused. We used rudimentary tools like the trowel, and we spent a lot of time thinking about diet and health. We researched plants for green manure, planned a sizeable worm farm and had a raft of ideas for energy conservation and experiments with wind and solar power. In effect we were practicing permaculture.

'Why not promote Voltaire's Garden as a model of permaculture?' Dave suggested.

'Because I don't like labels, especially when they are intellectual inventions that glamorise practical common sense,' Greg said, his tone defiant.

'But Greg, you could be missing an opportunity. Other people don't have your background. Vast numbers have lost their way. Some have no idea that beef comes from a cow.'

'And what about that girl at my school who won't eat home-laid eggs because they come out of chicken's bottoms. She prefers the one's from the supermarket,' Sarah said.

Everyone laughed.

'I think permaculture is all in the doing,' Greg said. 'You can study the book or do a course and you will have information in your head but permaculture is wisdom that can only be drawn out of experience. Information gathering is a vicarious form of knowing. Permaculture, like all creative ways of living and knowing, requires learning by doing. Besides, I can't stand labels!' He couldn't and he was emphatic about it.

The room responded with silence.

Greg went on. 'And I still maintain that all we are doing here is what any intelligent peasant the world over would do.'

'I see what you mean,' Dawn said, before navigating back to her earlier point. 'But don't under-estimate the work. A garden like yours is a lot of work. You will need help, eventually.'

She was right. I already had WWOOFers in mind, willing workers on organic farms, involving free board and lodging in return for labour. Greg though, he wasn't even keen on that idea. Yet Dawn and Ivan were right. We were staring into an untenable future if we kept on doing things Greg's way and remained hermits on the hill.

Time for dessert. I brought out a sticky orange pudding made with oranges from a neighbour's orchard. Everyone groaned.

Dawn was right about our need for community support for another reason. Extra hands at harvest and preserving times would always be welcome, but the major benefit was to counter the isolation that comes with working so hard. When we were both so busy it was too easy to forget that other people existed, or that we needed to connect with them. Over the last seventeen months we had barely had a social life. Greg said he didn't mind but I wasn't sure I believed him. I knew I need friends around me and that I had neglected so many since this project began.

Pushing isolation aside I continued to work hard, even when my own conviction that our project was waning through exhaustion played on my mind. And then there was the matter of climate uncertainty. There were droughts to get through. Hard times when communities pulled together. There was no telling what climate change would do to Australia and we were keen to protect ourselves from the worst effects.

In part, philosophy concerns itself with how to live our lives for the common good, and for us, this meant discovering a sense of purpose and fulfillment in the doing, in work itself, and in the physical processes that bring us close to, and in harmony with, the natural world. In *Candide*, Voltaire not only highlights the futility of abstract metaphysical searches for meaning and purpose of life through his juxtaposition of the slamming of the door in Pangloss's face by a Sufi dervish, with Candide's realisation of the value of work in the garden, Voltaire also emphasizes the point that wisdom is found through toil and the attention we pay to what is directly in front of us, and not in the abstract, metaphysical realm of ideas.

Humanity would do well to heed this advice, I thought, not only in terms of religion, but in terms of economics too. Humanity reaps the consequences of gifting impunity to a small group of super-rich individuals, an apparently amoral and unconscionably greedy elite who have little concern for anything other than their own acquisitiveness and do more or less as they please, even though these individuals have little regard for, or sense they are a part of, the wider community.

Voltaire, later in his life, affirmed the value of work, and of supporting his local community. He devoted the last twenty years of his life to social justice, in part through campaigning tirelessly on behalf of certain individuals unfairly imprisoned, and in his support of his local community, establishing a small silk industry on his estate and a watch-making industry in the nearby village of Ferney. He opposed unfair local taxes and raised the standard of living of all employees.

Voltaire carries his conviction into *Candide* in the final chapter, when Candide meets a Turkish farmer who, with just twenty acres and two daughters to help him, lives a very happy and simple life unconcerned with anything other than looking after the land he has. He works hard and is satisfied. Candide realises that the farmer has completed the answer to his search for meaning and happiness – don't concern yourself with questions too large and abstract, concern yourself instead with the work in front of you, which happens to be gardening. In other words, sowing, tending, feeding, watering and reaping in one endless cycle dictated by nature's rhythms.

The book ends at a beginning, our beginning. We'd taken Voltaire's advice both literally, by creating a garden and a place designed to support our basic needs, and metaphorically, as it did not escape our notice that the process of gardening was a wonderful metaphor for living a life.

A gardener cares deeply about the material she works with and its various needs; is flexible and adaptable to the requirements of that material in light of differing contexts and the vagaries of external conditions. Ideally a gardener compromises with the broader context of nature, taming, cultivating, and placing her particular stamp on nature's own processes without harming or destroying what is already there.

Gardening is universal work for a common humanity. We sow a seed, we watch it grow, we nurture it to fruition, and then we harvest, saving seed to plant next time. When we lose touch with this profoundly symbolic process in our lives and become cut off from this level of care in all we do, it does us good to return to the garden and begin to learn again a process we can then apply to our daily activities, whatever they may be.

It was all terribly idealistic and I lived that idealism with stoic conviction, unaware that it was all about to come to a sudden end.

CHAPTER SEVEN

FEATHERS AND FRIENDS

'If you could have come here this autumn, I should have tried to provide you with good food, simple rather than delicate.'

VOLTAIRE, IN *VOLTAIRE IN EXILE.*

Greg was dozing in the deck chair I'd put out on the grass in front of the courtyard. We'd enclosed the courtyard by erecting the two massive glass panels we'd acquired cheap as part of the same cancelled order that had supplied the pane beside the French doors opening into the living room. Gino and Damon helped Greg install the glass, and we'd centred a double sliding door to fill the remaining space, the result a seven-metre span of glass. The enclosed courtyard had quickly turned into a multi-purpose, seven by seven metre room, somewhere for our guests to mingle without entering the main house. Beside the glass panel to the west, two steps led up to the kitchen door. At the back of the courtyard, Greg had also made wide steps leading up to the French doors – re-purposed factory doors replete with metal mesh glass. Beneath the window opening into a small study in the east wall, Sarah had positioned her treadmill. The girls were sixteen now and while Mary had veered into jazz, Sarah was practicing yoga, working out in her bedroom and dragging me to the swimming pool at six each morning for laps before school, something I did willingly as I joined in, enjoying the cool water.

It was summer again. Where Greg sat dozing in his chair we envisaged a pergola for grape vines to help shade the glass. Beside him, in the garden bed below the kitchen windows, an enormous chili plant's pendulous fruit swayed in a light sea breeze. Basil bushes nestled between lemon grass, cardamom and tomato vines. Across the lawn, the fig tree burgeoned. Down by the dam, noisy mynahs squawked and cavorted in the old red gum. It was dusk and a summer haze captured the setting sun, giving forth a warm peachy glow.

I drank Greg in from my purview on the top terrace, before reaching for a clump of tarragon to accompany a handful of garlic chives and fresh garden mint for the evening's potato salad. In my side vision, I spied Pickles trotting over to Greg for a cuddle.

'The hard work's nearly over, *mon petit homme*,' I called out.

'I know, the home straight,' he called back wearily.

'Only three bathrooms and the weatherboards to go.'

'On the house? Maybe. But then there's the chook house, the fencing, the propagating shed, my workshop,' he said with a huge yawn. 'And no doubt a thousand other things.'

'And a great way of life to look forward to,' I said, trying to sound encouraging, knowing that my words had little effect on the way Greg felt. He was mentally and physically exhausted.

His face had lost its boyishness and taken on a dour, pained expression and there was a harsh intensity in his eyes. His lean torso was too brown, too weathered, and his hair was unkempt and standing in three distinct peaks, one atop and two to the sides. He looked like a blonde Oompa Loompa from Willy Wonka's chocolate factory.

We had another couple of years before the basic infrastructure would be finished and I wondered how we would manage to stay focused and positive. It would have to be me who injected the enthusiasm we needed to see us through. Greg's had run out.

When we'd arrived to live in the caravans some twenty months before, we faced piles and piles of dirt, rough patches of paddock, site cuts with unsightly batters, hundreds of metres of deep rips and a fetid-looking boggy mess in our transpiration bed. Now our trees and shrubs were in their second year of growth and, having survived the drought thanks to thick mulch, my assiduous watering program and the girls' help, they were powering. Through continuous mowing, we'd transformed the paddock into lawn. We'd created terraces out of the surplus top soil from the house cut and backfilled the batters with trash mulch. We'd landscaped grassy sweeps and created gentle arcs around garden beds. My random plantings of trees dotted around the house had defined possibilities for future large beds and intimate garden spaces. We'd cleared all the branches away from the main trunk of the fallen apple gum which looked magnificent on the saddle, its shape mirroring the roofline of the house from the driveway. It was a winning feature in its formal, native garden setting, the plants acquired using part of the Landcare grant.

Thankfully, too, everywhere was green. I'd come to love the endless cycle of mowing, raking, weeding and mulching, gradually expanding mulched circles surrounding each tree and shrub, circles that grew into oxbows, oxbows joining up to make garden beds, garden beds sporting ground covers and native shrubs with tiny, red, pink and white star-like flowers and bottlebrushes dripping nectar, sending happy bees into a delirious carouse. On the terraces, our red cabbages had swelled so enormously in the spring rains they'd attained the size of soccer balls, some weighing five kilos. We were drenched in abundance, the fruits of our labours, and we had a house that was nothing short of magnificent.

Three arms of the house stretched north, each with three long windows in the end wall sheltered from the summer sun by the eaves of a matching off-centred gable. At present, the walls were cement grey. Once Greg started on the weatherboards, I'd step in to paint the exterior. And then, with a few finishing touches, we could open for business.

Laden with produce, I approached Greg on my way to the kitchen. He'd fallen asleep so I nudged his foot. He didn't stir.

The girls were still up and about when we retired for bed after dinner, the summer dusk slowly fading into night. Soon we were serenaded by Mary playing *Moonlight Sonata* in her bedroom down the hall, accompanied by a choir of frogs, no doubt singing our praises for providing them a new habitat. The piano and the frogs made for a vibrant evening concert.

Greg started to breathe heavily with the occasional nasal snort.

We are all animals in our way, I thought, making noises, breathing and eating, living and dying.

He snorted again. I nudged his back. He turned and grew quiet. I lay beside him, listening to Mary and the frogs, drifting into the reverie that comes before sleep, wondering what to do with the red cabbages.

How different my world was from the life I'd led in England as a teacher, when my concerns centred on my physical appearance and how to make my personality fit a lifestyle of consumption, the daily routine, the continual back and forth from work to home, how to pay the mortgage and credit card and, in a more abstract way, how to contest dominant views and ideologies and models of the world in my classroom through my teaching.

I'd left England to live in exile and now my life had transformed. It was as though Voltaire's Garden had erased my former life completely. A metamorphosis had been silently occurring through the processes of doing, acting, behaving and working differently, foregrounding my core values, those that had always been present within me, but held in abeyance until this juncture. I had no idea if this new butterfly me would be permanent. But I wanted it to be. There was no going back to the life I had before. The conventional concerns I used to hold had slipped away. I wore whatever clothes I could find that were comfortable, loose and practical, and paid little attention to my appearance. I never visited a hairdresser, and I'd discarded my makeup. Self-esteem was now nurtured through myriad creative acts. I was what I did, not how I looked. Daily life revolved around the garden, the seasons, and how we could improve productivity. Consuming had become preserving and sharing, and thankfully at last, an increasing sense of community involvement. The abstract realm of ideas, ideologies, perspectives and models that directed our world and helped navigate us through it, had changed for me into a single point of focus on the natural world. My appreciation of the tremendous beauty of the landscape that surrounded Voltaire's Garden had fostered in me values of responsibility, care, nurture and frugality, of finding meaning and purpose in life through working in the garden.

Voltaire also exercised his passion for change in his garden. Even before he moved in to the chateau at Ferney, he began to improve the run-down estate. He had hedges repaired, ditches cleaned out and fields ploughed. He ordered five-thousand vine stocks and replenished the forest with partridges. He was no arm-chair gardener either. He had a special fondness for his cattle and would visit the cow-shed regularly. In renovating the garden, he provided employment and food for hundreds of workers. The seeds for *Candide* were sown in the process.

It seemed that Voltaire had taken an Epicurean turn. He delighted in fresh food and friendship, his chateau becoming a virtual drop-in centre for hundreds of invited and uninvited guests, many passing by on the Grand Tour of Europe. Through his exile Voltaire became a voice on the edge. After a lifetime at centre stage as a popular, if much criticized dramatist, he spoke out against judicial atrocities from the vantage of his retreat, and it was entirely due to his exile that Voltaire was able to exert such influence from a safe distance, his letters reaching politicians, monarchs, lawyers, doctors and others in positions of power or eminence.

Voltaire was a noble and impressive example, perhaps hard to follow, but I also knew that whatever your sphere of influence, you could change things. Maybe I, maybe we would follow in his footsteps in this remote corner of Australia.

The following day, from the dining room windows, I saw our neighbour John drive up in his ute. When I walked outside I found him in the garden talking with Greg.

I was about to offer John a red cabbage but he had other things on his mind. He'd come over to suggest a barter. He needed help with some fencing and in exchange offered to slash the wood-lot rips with his little tractor, which was just the right size for the job.

I felt so relieved I cheered a hooray. The grass in the wood lot was knee high and I'd been avoiding the challenge of mowing it with the two-stroke mower we'd bought to replace the one Greg killed mulch-making. It was a dreadfully difficult task for a woman of my build, requiring of me every skerrick of vigour and fortitude.

When John looked around at the recent progress in the garden he noticed a pair of wagtails teasing Pickles.

'We had a pair of wagtails hanging around our place, but now they've disappeared. I think our birds are migrating to your place.' He didn't sound too happy about it.

'Surely not,' Greg said, looking around.

'We had swallows too, but they've gone. It's a shame.'

I suppressed a smile, knowing the swallows preferred to perch in rows of ten or twenty along the ridgelines of our roof before taking off in flight. I loved their cute tawny torsos and triangulate wings, darting like batty torpedos.

John persisted with his observations over the defection of avian life to Voltaire's Garden.

'You haven't seen the black-faced cuckoo shrike?' he said.

I looked blankly.

Greg paused. He seemed to know the bird. 'No, I haven't.'

I took a mental note. I was not a bird watcher. In the middle distance, I still couldn't always tell one bird from another. Although I now knew we had a sizeable complement of avian life. We had magpies, which were obvious even to me; plovers who strutted about like serious men in dinner suits; a flock of white corellas, rumoured to be the product of a pair of local backyard escapees, their raucous shriek competing with the noisy mynahs, mynahs who screeched like mothers scolding children; we had galahs who loved to hang, swinging upside-down on branches and overhead power lines; several kinds of parrot sporting vivid reds and greens; and then there were the black cockatoos with their prehistoric cry. We had three kinds of wild duck, along with wrens, swallows, mud-larks, honey eaters, gang gangs, dollar birds, herons, chouffs, ibis, the ominous raven and the unwelcome starling. Then there were top-knot pigeons, kookaburras, owls, hawks, goshawks, kites and the wedge-tail eagle. Also the odd bower bird – the vegie garden decimator – and, Greg's favourite, the butcher bird, so friendly they easily became familiars. We even had a pair of little grebes, but apparently, no black-faced cuckoo shrike.

When John left I returned to the kitchen. It was looking magnificent now Greg had made and fitted all the doors and I'd painted them glossy white. A stone pine bench, lovingly hand crafted by Greg out of two thick slabs joined lengthwise, divided the room from the dining area, and faced a mulberry-coloured, Laminex bench housing the double sink. Wanting to continue with the Voltaire-inspired colour palette, I'd chosen black, mulberry and Dijon mustard wall tiles and, on the floor, commercial-grade vinyl tiles in pale green. The triptych of tall narrow windows over the kitchen sink looked directly over the orchard and past the tank at the old red gum by the dam. Separating the two styles of bench at the apex of the U was a commercial style, brushed-steel cooker. The U faced a large fridge beside a gigantic pantry. On the other side of the pantry were two tall bookcases filled two-deep with jars of preserved tomatoes, jams, pickles and chutneys.

It was a scene begging for some serious culinary action.

I was thrilled to be at last in a position to host a large dinner party. It was close to Christmas and we'd not celebrated anything in ages, so I decided to host a feast, a banquet, a ceremonial gathering to celebrate how far we'd come in relatively little time, and to acknowledge the hub of our life, the central point drawing to itself everything at Voltaire's Garden – our kitchen.

Keen to discuss the idea, I rushed outside to find Greg extending a garden bed outside the west wing where the girls' caravan used to be.

'Let's call this a milestone,' I said, as if he'd been privy to my musings.

'What?' Greg leaned on his garden fork, puzzled.

'The kitchen. I've wanted to have a dinner party for so long. Let's make it a feast.' I paused, waiting for a reaction. I didn't get one so I went on. 'I think we should have a big one. I'd like to have a feast for gardeners – our friends, the people who have supported us over the last two years.'

'When?'

He maintained a doubtful look but I refused to be defeated.

'Before Christmas.'

'Who will we invite?'

Suddenly, I wasn't sure.

'I'll write a list.'

Before I even had pen and paper ready, Charlie sprang to mind. His timber was so beautiful, straight and strong, and without it, we wouldn't have a house. Then there was Acko and his wife and keen gardener Kim, who I promised a dinner at our house some time ago. Patto and Gino had to come, as did Dave and Debra, who'd enthused about Voltaire's Garden from day one. We were also indebted to our friends Laura and Peter, and my employers at the post office Sylvia and Peter, who were also gardeners and appreciators of fine food. It was about time we reciprocated their hospitality. John and Hillary were a must, they were treasured neighbours whose spirit had jollied us along in a way they probably didn't realise.

Greg entered the kitchen for a glass of water.

'How many is that?' he said, leaning over my shoulder.

'So far, including us, eighteen.'

'How will we seat that many? And what do you mean, so far?'

'I've only just started the list.'

'I think you'd better stop there. We won't have enough chairs.'

His pessimism was beginning to irritate.

'We'll work something out. I'll see who can come, and if any are already committed elsewhere, I'll invite someone else.'

I wanted to invite the girls' friends too, especially Vanessa and Sarah and Polly, but I had to set limits. Dawn and Ivan and Gabrielle and Daniel would have to be back up guests too. Our respective parents were not a consideration. None of them would drive in the country at night.

It would not be eighteen guests if everyone came but twenty-two, as I wanted to invite Damon and his wife Julie, along with their children, Ella and Rhys. I also wanted to surprise Greg with a birthday party since his birthday was close to Christmas. Even grumpy drawers could raise a smile for that.

Later in the morning, after making many phone calls, I settled on a date, Friday 21 December, the summer solstice and three days after his birthday, a day when almost all our guests were available. Hillary would be in Sydney only days before, Laura had an appointment in Sydney on the very day of the feast but planned driving straight down the coast afterwards to make it, and Patto and Gino would be driving down from a trip to the Gold Coast the day before, but told me that our feast was all the reason they needed to return on time. Only Charlie had a prior engagement that he couldn't break, his daughter's twenty-first.

With the guest list settled, I planned a menu that once again made use of our own produce, building in a Mediterranean feel. I decided on dolmades and hummus as entrées, followed by marinated cubes of pork in a harissa style paste, fried off and served with coconut cous cous, and homemade cannelloni stuffed with spinach and ricotta cheese smothered in a rich tomato sauce. Both dishes would be served with red cabbage slaw, French bean salad, and salad greens tossed in olive oil and balsamic vinegar. Dessert will be Greg's birthday cake. The food would be rich, varied, and for the most part freshly picked. I asked half the guests to bring nibbles to start, and the other half, cheeses to finish.

All the food would be simple and wholesome. It was the flavour that counted, above all. Food should be plentiful and pleasing to the palate, satisfying for the stomach and nourishing for the body. The feast would be a symphony, delicately composed, with high notes, bass notes and many more between, in perfect balance and harmony. And just as an orchestra required a range of timbres to fulfil its function and satisfy the aural sense, so too did a feast, for the oral pleasure it gave to the supreme, discriminating sense: taste.

Before I began to invent a recipe for the birthday cake, the phone rang. It was Hillary, wanting to know what she should bring. I paused for a second, then tentatively suggested the cake. That way, Greg would have no idea the feast was also a surprise birthday party.

'I'd love to,' Hilary said. 'What kind of cake?'

'Chocolate?'

'I can make a very nice chocolate and beetroot cake if you like.'

'Wonderful! And I'll tell you what, I'll send Sarah over on the day with the ingredients for the icing. How does that sound?'

'Marvellous.'

Sarah was fond of Hillary and it would be good for her to have a role to play. Mary could help me set out the tables to make things fair. They'd rarely helped on the building site, much to Greg's continual irritation, or in the garden after their wonderful efforts with the watering. But they were teenagers and to their credit they always helped in the kitchen. Even though, at sixteen, both girls caused me enormous worry at times, they were always available and cooperative when I really needed them. Although, never when they believed my need was not that great.

The day of the feast arrived. We awoke early to face a warm and humid mid-summer morning. I leaped out of bed and began work in the kitchen before Greg had opened both eyes, excited and eager to start cooking in the cool of the day.

I heated milk for yogurt while making coffee, already planning and prioritising. I'd made a loaf of bread the night before and soaked the chickpeas. Greg appeared, taking up his usual seat at the dining table. He had his back to me.

'Any plans for the day?' I asked.

'I'll mow the dam wall and mulch the orchard.'

On his birthday feast? Then again, he didn't know that. And it was the most arduous of all our mowing duties, the dam wall steep and the kikuyu tall and thick, and if he didn't get to it soon, he'd get distracted by some other task and I'd be landed with the treacherous mow.

'And help with the harvest?' I said.

'Always.'

After breakfast, we picked strawberries, green beans, a big bag of vine leaves for the dolmades and a large bowl of spinach for the cannelloni. Back in the kitchen, I heated milk soured with lemon juice to make ricotta-style cheese, watching as it separated, then removing the curds to drain in muslin over the sink. Greg entered the kitchen with more spinach and a red cabbage.

By eight-thirty, the ricotta cheese was in the fridge and the vine leaves cooked. The chickpeas were boiling. For the dolmades I put rice, allspice, parsley, lemon juice, chopped almonds and raisins, along with salt and lots of black pepper in a bowl. The mix was ready just as Greg tried to escape into the garden again.

'Wait!'

'What?' he said, glancing at the clock, 'More coffee?'

'No time for that. I need you to make dolmades.'

I pointed to the vine leaves and the filling. I would have loved for him to be free to do as he pleased, but I couldn't prepare so much food alone. The dolmades required special care, not something I could entrust to the girls.

At nine-thirty, I tore into Bermagui for a four-hour stint at the literary agency. Four hours of dealing with emails, answering the phone, tracking contracts and filing. I was alone in the office that day and spent more time drinking in the view of Horseshoe Bay and Gulaga mountain than I did staring at the computer screen.

At two, I raced home to prepare the hummus. By then the kitchen was hotter and steamier. When Greg returned from the Cobargo pub with two of magnums of Aussie champagne, I got him to finely chop the spinach. Lightly steamed and mixed with the ricotta, a finely diced onion, eggs, nutmeg salt, pepper and grated parmesan, it turned into a squelchy, green-white goop for the cannelloni.

Making pasta dough was tricky. By now I was getting flustered. The dough needed to be kept chilled and the heat and humidity meant ice was called for when I mixed the dough, which should have been made the day before and left to rest in the fridge overnight. But time was running out and quantity overrode quality. It wasn't my best effort, I couldn't roll the dough thinly enough, but once made, the cannelloni would at least look nice lying on a bed of lemon sorrel, smothered in a rich, homegrown tomato sauce.

Thankfully the salad greens took no time to chop and dress with extra virgin olive oil and balsamic vinegar, but it took me an hour to slice the green beans, which I steamed, drained and dressed with olive oil, crushed garlic and black pepper. Then I made a huge bowl of grated red cabbage coleslaw.

When Sarah returned from icing the cake, she and helped Mary find chairs scattered through the house. We lined up several tables end to end in the centre of our living room, covered them in white linen, and then realised we lacked a matching set of crockery and cutlery for twenty-four. I couldn't imagine anyone would mind but made a mental note for the future.

I looked at the clock. It was ten to six.

I ran to get showered and changed, hoping for once that our guests arrived late.

No chance.

I was still buttoning up my dress when Peter arrived with an esky of drinks, a broad cheeky grin, and a seedling oak tree he'd potted up for a present.

'This is for you,' he said, handing Greg the little tree.

'Thanks.' Greg fingered the leaves and smiled.

Peter never wished him a happy birthday and he'd been talking of bringing us an oak tree for some time. Greg still had no idea.

John and Hillary arrived a few minutes later. Hilary had her foot in a large bandage. She was recovering from day surgery. During the greetings and introductions, John beckoned to Sarah saying, 'I'll just nip back to the car. I forgot something.'

Sarah followed him outside. I positioned myself beside Greg and Peter who were hovering at the other end of the long table, making sure to keep Greg's back to the door. A few moments later Sarah and John re-entered with the cake. My job of keeping Greg from turning around was made easy as he was deep in conversation with Peter about macadamias and self-seeding parsley.

Sarah marched through to the kitchen with the cake, John following to help her find room in the fridge. Greg was still oblivious. He looked past Peter and out the living room windows.

'More guests, Isobel,' he said, before taking a second look. His face lit up as he said, 'Hey, it's Damon and Julie!'

He turned to me with surprise. 'I had no idea.'

'I wanted tonight to be special.'

'It is.'

Greg was especially fond of Damon. He was in admiration of his musical abilities. Damon was a charismatic performer and Cobargo's own celebrity. The whole Davies family were a delight. Julie was a community-minded woman, working hard in myriad ways in support of a raft of local organisations and committees. I'd long admired her commitment and energy. Ella and Rhys were model children, polite and engaging, and they soon sought out Sarah and Mary and disappeared into another room.

Julie handed me a quiche for the children while Damon gave Greg an envelope.

'Just a small token of our esteem,' he said.

Greg looked puzzled for a moment, and as he opened the card, I leaned over his shoulder and whispered the words written inside.

'Happy Birthday.'

'Ah, Isobel.' He kissed my cheek. 'And you Damon, and Julie, thank you.'

In the next few moments our house filled with laughter and present opening, Dave, Deb and Ruby arriving as Peter and Sylvia, and Acko and Kim walked through the front door. Patto and Gino arrived a few minutes later, and our party was almost complete.

Everyone drifted through to the kitchen to deposit platters

and bottles of wine. The dining area was overflowing with guests and Mary and Sarah played hostess offering trays of nibbles.

This was the moment I preferred to leave Greg in charge, believing he was the one with all the social grace and confidence. I was so tired I felt awkward, not sure how to conduct myself, and the wine wasn't helping. It was probably my sheltered upbringing. I couldn't compete with Greg's glamorous childhood. I wanted to be a guest for a while, not a host, but this was Greg's day, so I had no choice.

Laura was the last to arrive, having made the seven hour drive back from Sydney in time to join us for entrées. Not long after her entry I heard light rain on the roof. It was just a shower. Laughing that she'd brought it with her, I told her what had happened to our floor on her fiftieth.

'You can't tell,' she said, glancing around at her feet.

Laura was distracted by Sylvia, who struck up a conversation about the post office, and the small matter of an overflowing mail box. As the community's chief bookkeeper, Sylvia kept her own counsel about most things and I was slowly getting to know her. A small, fair-haired woman with a winning smile, she exuded warmth beneath her reserved exterior. Laura carried a similar reserve, borne of many decades in a prominent role in a small community. The two women spoke in soft voices and I left them to it.

I found myself momentarily alone, observing the conversations occurring all around me, gazing past Julie and Debra to catch the flickering of late summer light on the old red gum. Voltaire's Garden was, as ever, magnificent. Surrounded by friends I'd known for several years and expected to know forever, I realised what a brave step it had been for me to commit, to Greg, to this land that now sported a home and a garden, and to the Cobargo valley with its old-fashioned charm and strong community spirit. Yet for all that, I sensed I didn't quite belong. The larger part of me remained an outsider looking in.

I found a sense of permanence only in trees, believing trees represented something fixed and immutable. A tree was rooted to the spot. All it could do was grow, flower, fruit and eventually die, its whole life spent right there where it began. Standing next to a tree I could feel its vibrancy. It gave nothing but life itself. It communicated, not in words, but in the way it stood, its shape, its texture, and the restricted movements it made in the wind. Whereas as people came and they went, taking a piece of my heart with them. Or rather, I came and went. I was the one who generally did the leaving. But not this time. The only place I planned on moving to was across the highway, the location of the town's cemetery. I was emphatic about that.

It might have been the wine doing my thinking for me, but right then I was certain there could be no higher purpose in a human life than what I had right in front of me, out there in the garden.

Without the special contact with nature that comes from gardening, we were all too easily de-humanised. Whether in pots on window ledges, in a tiny courtyard or patio, in a place like ours, or bigger still, the lessons were always the same, always there to be learned, taken back into the human world and applied to daily life. The garden was a place of nurture, and it was through the garden that I was able to show my friendship. Every person in the room that evening had received bags of vegetables from Voltaire's Garden.

Dave, who had taken a solo tour around the house and garden, entered the kitchen and walked straight up to Greg.

'Mate,' he said, putting an arm around his shoulder, 'I'm in awe of you.'

Greg was visibly flattered but I knew it was hard for him to take in. He was similarly in awe of Dave's role as Landcare co-ordinator, and his dedication to community building. Greg preferred a more solitary existence. Community, for him, was something he performed to, not participated in. He was a consummate actor.

Acko overheard the conversation.

'It's the last of an era,' he said in appreciation. 'Nobody builds like this anymore.'

'I think it's a mansion,' Deb said, clutching her wine glass to her chest.

I squeezed through the crowd and arranged bowls and platters of food on the stone pine bench, serving the main course buffet style. One by one our guests took a plate and piled it with food.

Greg took the head of the table, flanked by Damon and Dave. He looked small and far away and almost cute beside the two tall, dark-haired men, a little impish boy entertaining his birthday guests.

Conversation at my end of the table diverted my attention.

'It's great to have the space for so many people all sitting at the one table,' John said. He was seated opposite me. Hillary, who'd taken the foot of the table said, 'Far better than having people eating off their laps.'

'It reminds me of when the whole family would gather round at Nonna's,' Peter said.

'Every home should have one,' Acko said, looking along the table. 'A great big room to hold a feast.'

'You need a great big room to put one in,' I said with a laugh.

'And you know,' said John, looking around, 'the place looks old, as if it's been here for a century.'

I knew what he meant. Greg had a way of building things so they looked like they'd always been there.

'And it really feels like a home in here,' Gino said. 'Owner builders put a bit of themselves into their house, their character.'

I looked around and wondered what this place said about us.

'And an awful lot of hard work too,' I said.

Kim turned to me and said, 'And not just the house. Look what you've done to the garden, Isobel.'

It was the first time I had met Kim and I got the sense she was keen to include me in all the praise. It took another gardener to understand that a garden bed doesn't emerge out of nothing, that it takes years of digging, planting, weeding, pruning and watering.

Acko looked dewy eyed. I thought it was probably the wine. 'What's up?' I said.

'Oh, nothing,' Acko said a little wistfully. 'I was just thinking about building. It just sunk in that an everyday thing to me is really special for each person I work for.'

'Your roof was the best Christmas present we received last year, and the day you came and plumbed in our kitchen. Until that day we were still camping, even though we were living in the house.'

We'd been through so much to get to this stage of an almost completed house. So many little milestones.

Hours passed like minutes and it was time for the cake. After the happy birthday chorus that went on for a fair while thanks to Damon, I served Greg's birthday cake with a compote of strawberries and dollops of creamy homemade yogurt, accompanied by the two magnums of champagne. Greg stood and gave a little speech, saying what he always said; that a feast was what Voltaire's Garden was all about, good food and good company to share it with.

'And you. Voltaire's Garden is thanks to you, Greg,' I called out from my end of the long table.

'It took two,' he said, raising his glass. He was beaming. I hadn't seen him so relaxed and happy in a long time.

'I'll second that,' Kim said with quick glance in my direction.

We raised glasses to Voltaire's Garden.

We finished the feast with platters of local cheeses and fruits, and Sarah acted as barista for coffees. As the evening drew to a close, one by one our guests rose from their seats and helped to clear the table of dirty plates. It was midnight before our guests began to leave.

At last only Acko and Kim remained, along with Patto and Gino who were staying the night in our caravan. We gathered at one of end of the long table, struggling our way through the remains of the champagne. I looked across at Acko. Something about tonight had touched him deeply. He didn't want to leave.

The conversation drifted to climate change, and the pressure we were all under to alter our habits and conserve energy.

'I go around the house turning off light globes knowing that my action is nothing in comparison to the savings industry could make,' Kim said with frustration.

We all agreed.

Why was our culture so slow to adapt when sweeping changes were needed at the level of society itself, and not just at the level of each individual? Why was it that making money was seen as more important than making the future secure?

At least at Voltaire's Garden we would be safe.

Greg was not in the mood for politics. He burst into an old American song he'd learned as a child.

While Acko and Greg crooned through all the old songs of the 1950s they could remember between them, Patto reminisced about her first time as an on-site owner builder.

It used to be the case in Australia, back in the fifties, that people could buy a cheap quarter acre block, pitch a tent on it and build a house. These days local governments usually banned people from living on site while building. People rented instead. When Patto and Gino bought their first block in the bush up near Nowra they built a camp site before they built a house.

'The local town didn't like the people who camped on their blocks, but we camped in style. Running water, electricity, a proper little kitchen and a shower. But mostly people went feral. They had nothing.'

'How do people live like that?' I said.

No one answered. Instead a crash of thunder reminded us that another storm was building outside.

'I think we better take our leave,' Acko said, gripping the table with both hands as he stood. I assumed Kim would be driving. It was one o'clock when I saw them to the door and waved them off.

Now there were four of us. We chatted until three without realising the time and flopped into bed exhausted.

The following evening, as I reminisced on the night before, I determined that our feast was more about the future than the past. We were lying on our backs in our bedroom, the window open. It was dusk. The frogs had begun their chorus of throaty calls. Magpies chortled and a kookaburra made a last cry before bedtime. Distant high-pitched tweets contrasted with the chirrups and squawks of parrots. In the background we could hear Beethoven's *Pastoral* floating through from the radio at the other end of the house. Mary was up.

We would always think of Voltaire's Garden as a place that stood for values lost in the maelstrom of modern consumer culture. Voltaire, and Epicurus before him, knew the value and significance of good food, healthy living and the garden. Both held values that transcended cultural limits, speaking to the heart and the whole of humanity, speaking of vitality, Eros, the giver of life.

Voltaire's Garden felt alive that season, just as nature was alive, a place that stimulated the senses, enlivened the mind, enriched the heart and nourished the soul. We'd built a refuge, driven by a strong aspiration to transcend our Western cultural limits. We'd built a sanctuary for ourselves, and for others who felt similarly alienated by a banal, blandly packaged blanket of consumerism, aptly portrayed by the contemporary palate for exterior paint – all lifeless browns and greys.

'Human creativity,' I said aloud, 'is at its most beautiful when it harmonises with nature, drawing inspiration from something greater than itself.'

Greg was already sleeping.

It was a sunny Saturday in January and it was my birthday. We rose early as usual. The morning sun made the gum trees flanking the hills to the north glow orange. I stood in the living room beside the courtyard window, watching.

'What a gift.'

Life was getting a little easier and Greg seemed happier. His health was returning along with his wit. The weatherboards had arrived two weeks earlier, and thankfully so had his son, Jasper, who was now twenty years old and had filled out gracefully into manhood. Recently returned from a year working in London, he'd fancied trying his hand at building. Greg and Jasper had worked furiously nailing on weatherboards and finishing the outside of the house, while I followed close behind with a paintbrush after work at the agency. Today, however, was a day off, for me at least.

After mid-morning coffee, Greg took me to Cobargo to buy some special meat for dinner. We parked the car at the top of the street outside the supermarket and walked down to the butcher at the bottom of the hill by the bridge. The morning sun cast soft light on the brightly coloured facades of the old weatherboard and brick buildings: The bright orange of the old petrol station now an art gallery; the opal shop, dark pink with black trim; more orange across the street at the newsagency. A series of weatherboard façades in reds, oranges, pinks, yellows, greens and rich browns, and the soft foliage of myrtles greeted our eyes.

As we neared the bakery, Julie exited the bookshop next door with Ella and Rhys. We exchanged thoughts on fertilisers as Sylvia passed us on her way to the supermarket. Then our neighbour John crossed the street to say hello and had a brief discussion with Greg regarding the price and relative merits of gardening gloves. Further on, we waved to a number of acquaintances and nearly collided with Debra and Ruby in front of the post office. We crossed the road and spent half an hour browsing in a gift shop.

At home, I heard the dulcet sounds of Beethoven. Mary, her still enjoyed classical music, was practicing Erik Satie's *Gymnopédie No.1*. I put the meat in the fridge and stood by the kitchen sink, staring out the window in reverie. The back garden, full of small fruit trees, shrubs and fully-grown vegetables glistened vivid green under the summer sun. The fig tree was already huge and needed pruning. The little bay tree planted more than two years ago was now a healthy proud pendant of dense, dark green. The still waters of the dam shimmered under a soft breeze. In the red gum a pair of wagtails flew from branch to branch in noisy chatter. A magpie surveyed the terraces for grubs from its vantage point on top of a tall red gum post.

Mary had moved on to *Sonata Pathetique*. She liked the drama of it. I did too. As if in agreement the wagtails decided to give chase to the magpies. A small group of corellas screeched from the branches of an apple gum nearby. I looked down. Below the kitchen window my small crop of basil had grown to shrub-like proportions. Tomorrow we would eat pesto. And sometime in the future, I hoped we would combine our homegrown basil and garlic with our own pine nuts and olive oil, all grown in our own garden.

I pictured a small potting shed beside a greenhouse above the terraces where the clay pile used to be, and a rustic chicken coop encasing our two mulberry trees. Chickens loved mulberries. Over by the orchard imaginary bantam chickens scratched around. I pictured a pergola in front of the courtyard laden with grapes grown for the table. The sun would shine as it always did, and our trees would cast long shadows, darker shades of green. In the gully above the dam, two black faced sheep would graze on lush green grass. A network of narrow paths, some concrete, others gravel completed my vision.

I went outside, changed my shoes for old boots, reached for a pair of gloves and walked down to the terraces. I kneeled. I raised the trowel in my right hand and drove it into the soil.

Another day and another moonset on Murrabrine Mountain. Morning mist blanketed the valley. A magical way to start the day, it made me feel we owned a bit part in *Lord of the Rings,* after Jasper said the view reminded him of middle-earth. This place was clean, pure and safe. The people here were as gentle and welcoming as the land they shared. This was not a place for impatient, go-getting types. Here, light-hearted humour prevailed over adversity, an atmosphere of tolerance and acceptance working on the soul like balm, smoothing care-worn city wrinkles, the edgy ruffles caused by urban nonsense. The Cobargo valley had none of the harsh ruggedness of Australia's interior landscape; it was nothing like the outback and here people didn't need the same grit and determination to work in heat and dust. It was more a setting for *The Darling Buds of May*. It was the perfect place to live in exile, in retreat from the madness of urban living.

Jasper entered the kitchen and smiled a cheery good morning. I went outside to garden before the day warmed up. Walking towards the weeds on the batter behind the rainwater tank, I knew we hadn't tamed nature. I didn't believe anyone really could. The plant kingdom did its own thing regardless. The most we could hope for was to exert an influence, gently participating in the great unfolding growth as we satisfied our needs. Our relationship with the plant kingdom was still a game of chance, we rolled the dice and hoped to get a good score. Our relationship with the animal kingdom was barely any different, except that animals would interact with us in ways plants couldn't. We already had a love-muffin for a cat and now the magpies had decided to take an interest in us.

I was poised to attack another kikuyu runner. Up on the grassy bank a magpie strutted back and forth, foraging for worms and grubs, watching. Magpies had a reputation for swooping, sometimes taking chunks out of people's scalps, so I admired them with caution. I remembered as a child ducking in fear when passing a group of magpies nesting in a tree on my way to school in South Australia and Greg, at the age of seven, had once been unable to get to school because of swooping magpies. Our magpies didn't swoop, they'd already decided our gardening efforts were providing them with a free lunch. They would strut like the one above me, not far away, pause, look over and then peck the ground pretending they were busy. Sometimes they sat on top of a nearby post, keeping an eye out for food while I weeded. They even humoured my pathetic attempts at mimicking their call. They stopped, and listened and chortled back a little, with a bit of a 'Huh?' thrown in.

Finished with the weeding I collected a basket for the day's harvest and returned to the kitchen laden with vegetables. As the coffee pot steamed on the gas stove, I chopped kilos of tomatoes for preserving. Milk cooled for yogurt and the bread was baking. A large basket of under-ripe plums sat on the kitchen bench. The red cabbages were now producing side shoot nuggets by the dozen and we needed to find a way to preserve them. I trawled through recipe books. Jasper, who was staying with us in caravan annex, offered to help, and we embarked on a few experiments.

Firstly, we tackled the cabbage. I thought pickling was a good idea since Jasper was prepared to do the shredding. He had the patience to carefully slice kilos of cabbage into fine strips, eventually filling a large bowl which we covered with brine and left for a day.

Next, I made a half-sugar-and-vinegar-strength tomato and chili relish by accident, the result of forgetting the initial quantities. It turned out to be a great condiment, ideally suited to winter cooking. Finally, I invented a recipe for sour-plum chutney, which I later found a perfect accompaniment for stir-fries, curries and hearty winter stews, lending a bass note that lifted all the other flavours on the palate.

Watching Jasper at work in the kitchen, I wondered if he entirely belonged to his generation. Greg's influence in his formative years had touched and developed in him an appreciation of gardening and food. I recalled one year of my childhood, in 1974 when I was twelve, the year my parents had a house in Hamley Bridge, a small town in South Australia. Our home had an established garden, with quinces, grapes, mulberries and a magnificent blood orange tree irrigated by run-off from the septic tank. While my sister and uncle played elsewhere, I sat at the table in the cool kitchen, helping my mother and grandmother chop fruit for jam, listening to the radio and the ensuing discussions about politics and world affairs, fascinated by my grandmother's resourcefulness and creativity. Maybe I'd inherited her culinary ingenuity.

Jasper, like his father, loved to forage in the garden for salad greens, marvelling at the occasional fruits he found on our young trees. It was Jasper who tasted our first almond – we'd planted a small almond orchard down by the dam beyond the terraces – and when I cried in dismay at not having first pick he went outside to find me another, bringing it to me with a sheepish grin. How sweet and moist it was.

In his short stay with us, Jasper created some fantastic recipes. His speciality was salads. His salad of diced mild chilis and cucumber, with salad burnet, lemon sorrel and French tarragon smothered in a tart French dressing was delightful. With Jasper in the house, each night we turned our summer glut into a stately feast. Many nights I sat beholding eight dishes, each carefully prepared and beautifully presented, thinking we ought to open a restaurant. Char-grilled zucchinis, tzasiki, falafel, red cabbage coleslaw, potato salad laced with garlic chives, mint and tarragon, tomatoes oozing balsamic vinegar, roasted capsicums, and bush beans drizzled with olive oil, garlic and lashings of black pepper.

Jasper's involvement gave me hope that Generation Y would manage to share in our values. Mary and Sarah were proud to live this way too, even though it had meant sacrificing many of things their peers took for granted, things our lifestyle couldn't afford, like mobile phone credit, unlimited Internet use, concert tickets and shopping trips in the city. Instead, we provided a stimulating and healthy environment, one that hadn't escaped their friends' notice. Since we'd had a functioning kitchen, Mary and Sarah were allowed sleepovers and their friends all adored the fresh produce, marvelling at the flavours and asking for recipes.

Perhaps we could reach hearts through stomachs, as the saying went, and if this was what it took to turn heads in this techno-mad world, then I could think of no better way to go about it. Taste stimulates the imagination, it develops powers of discrimination, helps us to value things, and leads, ultimately to an understanding of perfection. Children today needed to find paths through an overloaded, over-cooked techno-world of information, a world that, ironically, provided a paucity of knowledge, and where important questions concerning the meaning and purpose of life were rarely explored.

Jasper left Voltaire's Garden before the tomato glut. I had gone into planting over-drive last spring and now I had to deal with hundreds of kilos of tomatoes. I made tomato sauce, tomato relish and tomato juice. I froze. I bottled reduced tomatoes for winter stews and sauces. Nine huge bowls of tomatoes adorned our kitchen benches for the whole of February and March. I phoned friends. They came. They loaded their cars with bags, buckets and boxes of ripening Romas to do the same at their place. I never asked for money. If a friend had something to give in return it was always welcome, but their gift to me was in the taking. Crazy Isobel had done it again, but if that was all I was guilty of, of being unable to restrain myself from growing too much, then so be it. I'd no intention of changing.

Even Pickles was having a bumper time.

One late-summer morning Greg dashed into the house.

'Quick, come and have a look at this,' he said, dragging me away from the tomatoes.

Outside, Pickles sat all proud with two bulging cheek pouches and a feline smile on her face, a wriggling mouse tail poking from each corner of her mouth.

'Remember those fifteen cheap, plastic, mouse traps I bought when we moved up here?'

'The one's we couldn't set because they kept going off.'

'We don't need them now, that's for sure.'

CHAPTER EIGHT

GENIUS LOCI

'But as an indefatigable reformer...he never ceased to preach that men had the obligation to make this the best world it was possible for them to make.'

PETER GAY ON VOLTAIRE.

One year later we opened for business. Our first guests were Gino's parents who'd come to Cobargo for his cousin's fiftieth birthday party, a country and western style bush bash on a farm on the edge of Wandella, under the contemplative gaze of Peak Alone. The moment his parents arrived they were captivated by the view and when Greg and I guided Gino's mother round our garden, she stopped in many places, scanning, studying and smiling, eventually telling us how envious she felt and how much she would have loved to have had a place like ours. After they left the following morning, we found Gino's father had tellingly left his pyjamas under a pillow. Whether it was the creamy chicken curry I cooked for them the night before, the homegrown strawberries they ate for breakfast, the room which was spacious, or the view over Wadbillaga and the tranquillity of the surroundings, they were reluctant to leave and promised to return.

It was a sentiment shared by all our guests, including a charming couple from Melbourne, who booked for one night and stayed for three. Another guest asked Greg if everyone who stayed with us ended up re-assessing their life.

We were thrilled by those early responses; it was our reward for years of hard work and it was enormously satisfying that through the gentle stimulation of the senses – the captivating views, tasty food, the chorus of birds and frogs, the sweet flower smells, of orange blossom and lavender – Voltaire's Garden reached people in places perhaps held dormant in busy, urban lives.

Ours was not a lifestyle for those wishing to escape daily chores and busy routines filled with manual labour, or for hermits seeking a solitary life. As we neared completion of the major building and infrastructure projects, we re-joined the community network beyond our immediate friends.

We added our names to the Tilba Food Co-operative, which thrice annually bulk-ordered organic grains, nuts, dried fruits and a wide range of other groceries, distributed by its members to fill individual orders.

Sunshine warmed my skin through the windscreen as we drove north to the School of Arts Hall at Central Tilba to help sort my first delivery; when Greg had lived in Tilba he was a co-op regular. The drive was a pleasant one, coursing through tall forest that opened out at the base of Gulaga mountain. A herd of Jersey cows chewed lush grass. The tiny historic villages of Central Tilba and Tilba Tilba nestled under the mountain, their brightly painted weatherboard houses just visible from the highway.

We parked outside the hall, and entered large wooden doors to confront boxes and sacks forming a large cluster near the entrance. Beyond them, three rows of long tables arranged with scales and bags displayed the task ahead, and lining the walls nametags indicated the location for each order. The hall was filled with volunteers, including Damon's wife Julie, who had her laptop open on a small administration desk set to one side to attend to the bookkeeping. Ella and Rhys were with her, along with many other children.

I lost Greg in the throng and decided, after receiving a brief explanation of procedures, to distribute soy milk and a range of other goods that didn't need to be weighed. After managing to dodge by the tables stacked with boxes and sacks in a seemingly endless back and forth, I chose to tackle the nuts. I carried all the nut boxes to some unoccupied scales at the far end of a bench. Then I collected the relevant distribution dockets. I looked across the table to see Greg divvying-up one hundred kilos of organic sugar. Opposite him Debra had the light but bulky task of apportioning wheat flakes. Beside me an elderly gentleman carefully sorted liquorice. Soon he disappeared, replaced by a younger man tackling dried fruit.

I worked furiously and continuously, determined to see everything distributed as soon as time allowed, so that we could collect our order and go home. Hours passed and helpers drifted in and out, chatting, laughing and gently chiding children who had taken to running in circles screaming. As I worked I became annoyed. Everyone, I decided, ought to be working as hard as me. To speed up my process even more, I enlisted the assistance of first young Ruby, then Rhys, who proved to have an intelligent ability for distribution for his age.

Eventually all the nuts were in bags and placed in their

correct locations, and I took a short break, seated on a stool with a bottle of water. Greg walked towards me, having finished the sugar.

'How long before we can take our order and go home?' I asked quietly, raising the water bottle to my lips.

'We can't take it now,' he said. 'The orders have to be checked first. We'll come back after seven tonight, when they've finished.'

I sputtered, narrowly avoiding spraying water across the floor. I'd had no idea. Thinking fast, I managed to arrange with Julie an alternative that didn't involve us driving back to Tilba.

Later, Linda, one of the coordinators, gently explained to me that while it was lovely to see Greg and I work so hard for so long, it was not necessary, and really, people came to socialise a little. It was a wake-up call. We had been locked in a groove of hard labour for far too long. While those around us were chilling and enjoying each other's company, I'd been an express train. Next time I'd sort the liquorice.

The trouble was, everything we did at Voltaire's Garden involved hard work of some kind.

Julie delivered our order the following day, arriving as Greg was wheeling a barrow of rocks from the granite outcrop. They met over by the garage and I left them to it, returning to the kitchen to deal with the strawberry glut.

Greg was using the granite to form part of another rock wall. For several years, the outcrop had been the repository for Greg's stack of woodturning timbers and old corrugated iron sheets, and until recently, we paid it little attention. A few weeks ago, Greg had attempted to remove a boxthorn from the outcrop's lower edge, when he made a pleasing discovery – beneath the rocky soil were piles of granite rocks ranging in size from granular through to bread-sized boulders. Mixed between the rocks was soil comprised of rotted cow manure and granite dust. From that moment we hoed, raked, shovelled, barrowed and sieved using an old bed base to collate the various sizes of rock and separate them from the soil. We soon had our own little quarry, the result of a hundred and fifty years of land clearing by farmers. I was taken back to my 'sodding days' next door, when my parents had me picking up cow pats.

Originally, the land was strewn with granite, lying on the surface and nestling just beneath, an annoyance to farmers seeking to plough or slash paddocks for grazing. Now we were relocating the rocks again, to form retaining walls and rubble drains, and using the rich soil as top dressing on garden beds.

Greg appeared, carrying in the co-op order to the kitchen. I was confronted with twenty-five kilo sacks of flour, along with bags of nuts, grains and dried fruit poised to join an already overflowing pantry.

'I see I have some fun ahead of me.'

'You'll manage.'

'I've been thinking about Voltaire again,' I said before he disappeared outside. 'You remember how he paid attention to food, to ingredients, to quality and freshness, to the health benefits of herbs and how food should be prepared in simple ways.'

He paused in the doorway. 'And?'

'When you walked in with all that flour I immediately thought how lovely it will be when the elderberries come. I imagine elderberry pie made with organic wholemeal flour and homemade butter for the pastry, and served with creamy, lemony ricotta cheese. Which is fresh, quality food, healthy and simple, just like Voltaire would have wanted it.'

'Go on.'

'And the unexpected ways we find ourselves walking in his boots. Did I tell you he liked to stroke his cows? Anyway, the similarities are striking. Sometimes I feel as if the spirit of

Voltaire is here with us or something, infusing this place with his will, filling the atmosphere with his charisma.'

'The genius loci,' he said slowly. 'I've always wanted to give that name to some place in my life. Thank you for that.' He held my gaze. 'This place is the genius loci of the spirit of Voltaire.'

He smiled as he headed back outside.

Names are powerful, I thought, they breathe meaning into a thing, colouring, shaping, even dictating the bounds of what is and is not acceptable under its banner. In naming our property Voltaire's Garden, it was as if we both wore a new uniform, finding ourselves performing the actions the name seemed to imply or represent. With the passing of time we had taken on some of the characteristics that our new Voltairean uniform called for, the particular attitudes, values and ways of doing things. Yet the name Voltaire's Garden represented an amalgamation of two lifetimes of accumulated aspirations, along with a wide range of skills and talents we shared between us. We fitted the uniform well, because we were already wearing the template. Would either of us ever take that uniform off?

For Greg, Voltaire's Garden was more than an escape from the madness of a consumption-driven world; it was a form of protest. He wanted to live as simply and justly as he could, providing to all who visited an example of a different way of life, one open to future possibilities to foster change.

I saw it more as a metaphor and humanity needed new metaphors for living, new attitudes and values, fresh ways of viewing the world. We needed more transparent, honest and well thought through policies and models that were continuously evaluated and modified in the light of new discoveries and ideas. The current economic crisis of 2008 revealed how dangerous it was to invest all our faith in a simple and false assumption, such as the non-existent invisible hand of a neo-liberal model of economics.

A model is in essence a metaphor, a set of descriptors arranged in a particular pattern that has some explanatory power. Greg, who would often talk about creating a new political party, the Garden Party, contended that the world economy would benefit from considering the contribution the model of the garden could make to the development of new or existing theories: Put simply, a garden is a bounded infinity in which processes occur in patterns and cycles of birth, life, death and decay. Human action was vital to maintain a constantly productive and changing environment ultimately through tilling, weeding, planting, watering, tending, harvesting, pruning, and ultimately caring.

For me, these words are metaphors depicting ways of behaving, and I find the actions the words implied potently transformational. When we embrace the metaphor, like magic, something happens inside us, and before we have begun to understand how this could be, a change occurs, a shift in perspective, an engagement in hard work that brings contentment as if we know, deep down, that these words, these processes, are all we need to be happy.

Nothing brought me closer to the whole world than working in the garden and growing food. Through gardening, I touched a deep vein common to all humanity, the need to eat to survive and to have a sense that the economic fundamentals by which we lived were sound. It was another kind of spirit, an essence, something necessary, something sufficient. To forget about soil, I decided, is to ignore our own roots embedded in it, and to do that is to ignore our own depths of being, and to ignore this in turn is to ignore that which connects us to everything. The will to live, to be, to exist, the ultimate purpose of life, the question on a religious believer's lips, *is* the will of the planet itself. The more we stray from this basic truth, the worse off we are.

At Voltaire's Garden I was happy to eschew Western industrial life to be a peasant, a small freehold farmer or gardener, and therefore unite my soul with peasants the world over, not least my dearest Ghanaian teachers and friends.

It had taken me a long time to feel I belonged again after leaving England, my old school, the Ghana Link. It had been a tremendous loss. I had thought I would never again find myself in a situation in which I could have so great an influence on issues of fairness and justice. I was pleased to discover my successor continued in my shoes. She took the link to new heights. She met the Ghanaian president and addressed the House of Commons and the House of Lords in support of school linking. The Polesworth-Pampawie link became a model of excellence. She wrote and told me the school in Pampawie had erected a plaque with my name on it in their garden.

Genius loci.

I stared at a tropical garden abundant with thriving trees, shrubs and grasses. In the centre of the garden were two large semi-circles of raised concrete, their sides brightly painted in vibrant blue. On the surface of each semi-circle was a painting of a flag, one British, one Ghanaian. I no longer recalled where the idea came from, but I was pleased to find the concrete sculpture there.

I closed the Internet, shut down the computer and headed outside. It was a hot, steamy January and thunderheads were forming over the mountains. I saw Greg wheeling a barrow of weeds and joined him after locating my trowel.

EPILOGUE

All was not for the best in the best of all possible worlds. Six months later, the hard work broke us. I am not sure who broke first. I'd already stopped working for Mary at the literary agency, after finding the stress of my over-burdened life too much. Greg didn't slow down and it became clear to me he'd worked himself into the ground. I had worked myself into the ground. Voltaire's Garden lost its ethos and our beautiful lifestyle, along with all my hopes and dreams, vanished.

In the winter of 2009, I walked out on our broken marriage and headed to the Dandenong Ranges in Melbourne's outer east. It took me a long time to recover from the loss, the shattered dream. I wasn't sure I ever wanted to see a garden again, let alone create one. Optimism had given way to grief and I took up lap swimming in the local pool to get myself through it.

Gradually, I set up a new life and made many new friends, all of whom had been scarred by the events of Black Saturday. Friends described their experiences of that day. They mourned those who had died. I listened to their stories. Stories of frantic evacuations, choking smoke, intense heat and fear. I could scarcely take the recollections in. It was surreal to have relocated to an area so recently damaged by the fires. I had left behind another broken dream and come face to face with other people's horror.

I drove through the fire ground around the small town of Kinglake one day and saw for myself the blackened earth, the dead trees, others struggling to come back to life.

About a year later I bought a house in Cockatoo, a town that had been razed in the Ash Wednesday fires of 1983. Cockatoo nestles in a steep-sided densely wooded valley. If you drive through the town, you would not know anyone lived there; all the houses are obscured by towering mountain ash. I lived there for over three years, leaving after yet another summer of unease whenever the temperature rose and a dry north wind blew.

It was only after I returned to the Bega Valley, a part of the world I feel strongly connected to and dearly missed at the time, and settled into another new life in Quaama, a little town ten kilometres south of Cobargo, that I was able to read Adrian Hyland's *Kinglake 350*, a memoir of a policeman struggling to deal with the fires on Black Saturday.

I took little heed of the fire that had charged towards Quaama only a few months earlier, a fire that had seen my neighbour standing on her roof with a hose. That fire, which started on a farm in Yowrie on the other side of Mount Dumpling, had been lit by farm machinery. Just an accidental spark. The Rural Fire Service managed to put out the blaze. For the whole time I lived in Quaama, I would gaze out my kitchen window at the forest of Wadbillaga thinking that fire had been a one-off, and a conflagration would never devastate all that lush rolling green and forest wilderness. The fire fighters would come and put it all out.

The garden of my Quaama house sloped steeply downhill and faced northwest. The kikuyu grass loved the sunny aspect, making mowing arduous. The previous owner had created a row of garden beds along the side fence. From day one, I planted an assortment of vegetables, planning on keeping myself self-sufficient in produce. I contemplated chickens. But the injury I acquired that day I stepped off Greg's bathroom platform had other ideas. It turned out I had a couple of bulging discs in the lumbar region of my spine. Gardening involved bending and bending aggravated the bulges. So did using a fork or a spade.

Firewood was my other ordeal. Someone had thought it okay to situate the woodshed downhill of the house. I had no choice but to store the wood in the shed and barrow it uphill to feed the woodfire. Ross Rixon, the man who delivered my firewood, found my situation hilarious.

Ross was a local institution. I had known him for decades and worked on the agricultural show with his daughter June and his son-in-law Richard Tarlinton, who was president of the show committee when I was secretary. The Tarlintons are a large family mostly based in Wandella, a locality below Peak Alone west of Cobargo. A Tarlinton ancestor was Cobargo's first settler, having made the arduous journey down the mountains in search of grazing pasture for his cattle during a drought. I always thought that privately Ross was proud June had married into the family. A good-natured soul, Ross knew all about wood and how to cut it. And he was a real charmer. He would turn up at my place, dump a back tray of firewood and then hang around for a long chat. Whenever I mentioned having to barrow the wood up to the house he would laugh and tell me how he saw 'Trish the osteo' every other week to sort his back out. He was eighty-one years old.

I lacked Ross's robust strength, his resilience. I found the garden and firewood all too much. I sold up and moved again two years later with a heavy heart, realising going back was not the same. I was not the same. My interest in gardening was waning, the result of a sore back and a burgeoning writing career. I was pursuing another, sedentary passion, one I had held close my whole life.

By then, my daughters were both living in Melbourne. Greg had relocated too.

I left just before the start of a drought. A drought that would endure for three years. The day before I departed once more for Melbourne, I was seated with Laura in a café in one of those charming weatherboard buildings situated between the post office and the old bank, when the new owner of Voltaire's Garden approached me. I knew her. One time I had paid her a visit to see the old place. We took tea in the courtyard. It was a short visit. I couldn't fight back the tears.

In the café, she grinned down at me and announced that after five years of contemplation over the problem she'd finally brought in a bulldozer to flatten all the vegetable terraces. I knew she was only referring to all the hard work those terraces took to maintain, but I felt I'd been kicked in the guts. Knowing the terraces no longer existed ruined my fond memories of them. Of their astonishing fecundity, the result of years of hard labour. It was a kind of death. I couldn't have known it then that much worse was to come.

On 18 March 2018, when the fires raged through the seaside town of Tathra about sixty kilometres south of Cobargo, I was living in Warrnambool on Victoria's southern coastline where the predominant weather pattern brought moisture and rain. My parents were by then living near Tathra in the next town south. It was with much concern and sadness that I watched the news and read the unfolding story of the Tathra inferno through friends on Facebook. Sixty-five homes were razed in that fire. I read recently that reconstruction has been slow. The area does not have the resources to suddenly rebuild.

On 30 December 2019 the unthinkable happened. I'd been taking a keen interest in the fires after the blazes in the Blue Mountains west of Sydney coursed through areas I knew. I kept hearing Bell's Line of Road and pictured myself driving along it. All the fires raging around the whole nation seemed to have occurred in places I knew or had some connection with. I was on high alert that December day as the fires in East Gippsland were threatening the setting in one of my novels. I had researched the area thoroughly and as the fires charged through the forest and various locations were announced, locations near Mallacoota, I pictured my characters fleeing for the beach.

The stream of news from Victoria was interrupted by an announcement that a fire which had started up in the high country near Badja Road and not too far from Conway's Gap on the edge of Wadbilliga, a fire started by dry lightning, had turned into an inferno creating its own thunderstorm. Cobargo and the surrounding area were put on alert. I, too, was on alert.

But no one could have anticipated what would happen next.

The fire thunderstorm happened in late afternoon. After that, strong winds, a warm night and very dry air allowed the fire to traverse about twenty or thirty kilometres in a few hours. Evacuations started in the early hours in dense smoke as fires bore down from the mountain tops. I awoke on New Year's Eve to find that friends had been shunted from town to town to various evacuation points. Firefighters and those who stayed to defend their homes and properties faced a wall of flames charging through the valley, sending huge balls of fire rolling and bouncing down the hillsides. These fire bombs sucked the oxygen from the air, exploding trees and shattering all in their path and leaving a charred smoking wasteland in their wake.

The blaze was unstoppable. All the firefighters could do was watch as the inferno tore out a chunk out of Cobargo's main street before charging through the town razing houses in its path. They managed to defend the post office.

Those taking shelter in the local pub took photos that reached the headlines of international newspapers. I read every article. I watched all the footage. I caught up with every single person I knew by jumping on their Facebook profiles. My old home town Cobargo, no more.

It was trauma at a distance. Trauma that in time would fade. The real trauma was suffered and is still being suffered by those who got caught up in the inferno. Those fleeing in terror as flames lashed the roadside. Those whose houses and properties were flattened. Those who were burnt as they stayed to defend. Those who've lost their loved ones. And their animals.

Over sixty properties were razed around Cobargo in those few hours. Day after day, news filtered in from personal friends who had lost everything. I knew the men who had died. I worked with Robert Salway when I was secretary of the show society and my daughters had gone to school with his son Patrick.

My mother's old farm next door to Voltaire's Garden, the one she'd bought on her return from England, was flattened by the fire. Front page news featured the new owner standing in front of what was left of Mum's old bedroom. The farmer at the back of us lost a herd of two-hundred Black Angus cattle.

The house at Voltaire's Garden survived, although I have no idea in what condition. I do know the caravan complex and laundry-cum-bathroom were razed. I also suspect the wood lot I had slavishly planted between the caravans and my parents' farm contributed to the destruction of their old house. And the surrounding area will never be the same. Wadbilliga will never be the same. The birds, the wildlife, the habitat have been decimated.

Patto and Gino lost everything as did all of their friends. John and Sonia Evans saved their property. Peter and Sylvia had moved away but the local fire fighters saved the post office. John and Hillary lost all of their infrastructure – sheds, tanks – but their house survived. Dave and Debra, who lived in town, were spared. Peter and Laura's house survived after Peter stayed to defend, but they lost most of their infrastructure. He took footage of the fires lapping at the edges of his property before the communications went out. I spent an anxious few hours not knowing if he was dead or alive.

The fires had thrust me back into the heart of the Cobargo community. Not just Cobargo but the surrounding area including the village of Quaama and the localities of Brogo, Yowrie, Wandella and Coolagolite. Three weeks after the conflagration, when news articles announced on my birthday that an unnamed eighty-four-year-old man had died from his burns, I thought immediately of Ross Rixon. I have no idea why but I expected it to be him. I didn't want to be right. The next day I discovered I was. Cobargo had lost dear old Ross Rixon in the most undeserved and horrific way, and the heavy weight I had been carrying in my heart got that much heavier. Tears sat ready to spring forth at the slightest provocation. Sweet memories of a place I had held dear my whole adult life would carry the scar of 31 December 2019 forever.

And still the fires continued. The Badja Road fire burned through the whole of January, joining other fires to the north and south and forming a long band of fire ground all the way up to Newcastle and beyond. At the time of writing, the fires in Victoria's East Gippsland looked set to merge with those on the coast of New South Wales, and the fires in the high country including the Snowy Mountains had also formed vast fire grounds. The scale of the fires is hard to imagine. On bad days when hot winds blew from the northwest, old fires flared up again, sending ribbons of fire towards the coast, threatening all the pretty seaside towns on a two-hundred kilometre stretch of paradise, including Bermagui. Just when I thought it was all over, the weather would turn and the fire had another go at decimating the entire area.

To lose to fire your home, your livelihood, your animals, your farm is unthinkable and Cobargo, like all the towns devasted by fire, will never forget what happened there. Stories will be passed down through the generations. People affected will re-live those harrowing and terrifying moments for the rest of their lives. Many have been traumatised. The community itself is traumatised.

While the emergency and disaster and recovery efforts were underway, while those on the ground exhausted themselves trying to pull things back to some kind of post-apocalypse normalcy, while journalists and commentators discussed the various angles, while Australia as a nation battled with its own conscience and our fossil fuel fixated politicians continued to deny the root cause of climate change, while all that raged around me, I resurrected this little memory of Voltaire's Garden composed between 2007-8.

After donating all I could afford to various crowdfunding campaigns, re-visiting this memoir of my old life was the only thing I could think of to do that would help me process the impotent way I was feeling. Help me deal with my despair. I felt an urgent need to re-capture what had been lost, what was and is so special about rural communities in Australia and no doubt the world over, and to reflect on the bitter irony that it is those who are working hard to lead simple lives, those who do not pollute, those who are part of the solution and not the problem; it is those people who have been impacted so horrendously by these fires.

The fires that charged throughout Australia for five months in the spring of 2019 and through the summer, razed an area about the size of England. Fires so intense they created their own thunderstorms. Thunderstorms sending dry lightning many kilometres ahead of the fire front, lighting more fires. Thunderstorms generating fire tornadoes able to flip a ten-ton truck. It was an apocalypse. There is no other word for it.

Cobargo is a resilient little town and I know it will bounce back. Regional Australia is filled with little 'Cobargos', highly supportive communities rallying to help each other out. But it is imperative that the world acts on climate change, or eventually, not too far away, there will be no bouncing back, at least not to how things were. As it stands, regional Australia must adapt to the changed climate, whatever that may mean. Halcyon dreams no more.

My dearest wish is that this tragedy will foster in all of us the impetus to change our ways, change our governments' ways and those of the fossil fuel industry, lest what we witnessed in Australia in the 2019-2020 fire season be repeated year on year along with all the other extreme climate-changed events destroying lives and habitats. Perhaps humanity needs a touch of the wisdom of Voltaire.

RECIPES

Chicken and Tarragon Salad

Ingredients

One whole fresh chicken
2 bay leaves
several sprigs of fresh thyme and rosemary
a handful of marjoram
2 large onions
2 large carrots
2 celery sticks
salt, and a good dash of Worcestershire sauce
Enough water to just cover the bottom of the pan about two
centimetres

For the salad:

200ml homemade mayonnaise (eggs, French or Dijon mustard,
apple cider vinegar, lemon juice, good oil)

decent handful each of fresh tarragon, basil, and garlic chives, chopped finely.
couple of tablespoons of sliced pickled cucumber (can use some capers too), chopped finely
4 cloves of very fresh garlic, crushed
1 finely diced onion

Method

The day before, put the chicken in a large pot with a heavy lid, along with the vegetables, herbs, salt, sauce and water. Cover, bring to boil, turn down very low and allow the chicken to steam until it falls from the bones. Set aside the juice and vegetables for a tasty soup. Allow chicken to cool and refrigerate.
Mix all the salad ingredients together. Dice the chicken and add to the mix. Enjoy.

———

Pesto

Ingredients

2 good handfuls of fresh basil leaves (or cups full)
4 cloves of very fresh garlic (which really means home-grown)
50g pine nuts (or macadamias, or 50/50 of both. You can also use almonds)
½ teaspoon sea salt or iodised salt
50g grated parmesan (or romano, or a combination of both)
A quantity of the best extra virgin olive oil you can find

Method

If you have a large pestle and mortar, use it, otherwise place first the basil, then the other dry ingredients into a food processor. Add a good dollop of oil. Blend for a few seconds and check consistency. Keep adding oil in stages until the mix is a coarse paste that just slides off a metal spoon – not too thick, not too runny. Scrape out into a nice bowl and add a thin layer of olive oil if not serving immediately, to prevent oxidation and flavour deterioration. Perfectionists say the fast whipping of olive oil and garlic change their flavours, so out of caution, I blend the pesto for the shortest time on the lowest speed possible to do the job.

———

Green Lasagne

Ingredients

for the pasta:
400g oo flour
4 eggs
salt

for the fillings:

1 A large bunch fresh spinach, finely chopped (any beet, perpetual spinach, Australia's native warrigal greens, English spinach, lemon sorrel, in any combination)
freshly grated nutmeg and freshly ground black pepper

2 Four fat or eight thin leeks, finely chopped (include the green as well as white leaves), one bay leaf, a knob butter and one egg

3 Medium bowl of fresh snow peas (mange tout), cut in
quarters – can use fresh or frozen garden peas, a green lettuce,
shredded; 2 tablespoons of chopped herbs (marjoram, thyme,
tarragon, chervil, parsley in any combination)
salt

for the sauce:

butter and oil – several tablespoons
heaped tablespoon plain flour
teaspoon English mustard, freshly ground black pepper, bay
leaf, milk, salt
250g mature cheddar, grated; Parmesan cheese

Method:

To prepare pasta place flour and salt in a large bowl or on
bench. Make a well in the centre and add beaten eggs. Mix into
a stiff ball. Be careful not to overwork dough. Cover dough and
chill for an hour or more.
Steam spinach in a minimum of water until wilted but not too
cooked. Drain, keeping liquid, add nutmeg and pepper and set
to one side uncovered. Steam leeks in a little water with bay
leaf, again until only just tender. Drain, keep the liquid and
add butter. Place lettuce in a saucepan and then snow peas.
Add a little water and steam for a couple of minutes until
lettuce has wilted, but snow peas are still crunchy. Drain,
keeping liquid, and mix in herbs and salt.
Heat oil in pan, add flour and stir vigorously until combined
into a roux. Add milk in increments, working it in to the roux,
stirring continuously. When enough milk is added to make a
thick sauce add the other ingredients and the vegetable waters.

If the sauce is still too thick, add more milk. Cook for a few minutes and add cheese.

Place spinach in a blender or food processor, with the egg and whiz into a fairly smooth paste.

Roll pasta dough into thin oblong sheets to match the size of baking dish. The sheets should be quite thin. To assemble, place some snow pea and lettuce mixture in baking dish, cover with some cheese sauce, add a sheet of pasta, then some leeks, spinach, more cheese sauce, another sheet of pasta and so on until you completed the layers, reserving some cheese sauce to cover the final sheet of pasta. Sprinkle with parmesan and bake in a moderate oven for forty-five minutes.

————

Sour Plum Chutney

Ingredients

3kg sour plums
3kg sour apples
½kg onion
250g sultanas
4 cloves garlic
Allspice (a heaped teaspoon), coriander seed (several teaspoons), 1 cinnamon stick, 3 bay leaves, 15 cloves
6kg sugar
teaspoon salt
1 litre white vinegar.

Method

Chop fruits and onion and place in a large wide-based pan. Cook gently until liquid covers base of pan and then bring to boil. Stir and do not cover. Allow to cook until fruit is soft. Add spices, salt, garlic and sugar. Stir and cook to reduce liquid. Add vinegar, stir, and reduce until desired thickness. Spoon into clean jars and seal.

———

Jasper's Zingy chili Salad

Ingredients

1 long green cucumber
a medium bowl full of a combination of salad burnet, lemon sorrel, rocket and nasturtium and basil leaves
several sprigs of French tarragon
7 mild chilies
any combination of capsicum, tomato, peach, plum or nectarine
wholegrain mustard
½ teaspoon of sugar and of salt
1 clove crushed garlic
30% extra virgin olive oil to 70% white wine vinegar

Method

Finely dice cucumber, chilies, and fruits and place in a large salad bowl. Finely shred green leaves and add to bowl. Finely chop tarragon and add. In a clean jar with a screw-top lid place sugar, salt, mustard, garlic, oil and vinegar and shake. It will not emulsify as it has too much vinegar. Add to salad just before serving and mix well.

ACKNOWLEDGMENTS

I would like to thank all my Cobargo friends who supported me in writing this book. There were many others in my life back then, friends I was and am very fond of who due to the constraints of the narrative did not make the cut. A special mention to Rosemary Beaumont who put me on to the School of Social Ecology where I undertook my PhD. There is always so much more that can be said in a memoir.

My warmest gratitude to my mother for reading this manuscript and offering her opinions.

Two book consulted in the composition of this memoir:

Voltaire, *Candide*, first published in France, in 1759, Cramer, Marc-Michel Rey. The edition I used was released by Simon & Schuster, 2005.

Ian Davidson, *Voltaire in Exile*, New York, Grove Press, 2004.

Dear reader,

We hope you enjoyed reading *Voltaire's Garden*. Please take a moment to leave a review, even if it's a short one. Your opinion is important to us.

Discover more books by Isobel Blackthorn at

https://www.nextchapter.pub/authors/isobel-blackthorn-mystery-thriller-author

Want to know when one of our books is free or discounted? Join the newsletter at

http://eepurl.com/bqqB3H

Best regards,

Isobel Blackthorn and the Next Chapter Team

YOU MIGHT ALSO LIKE

You might also like:
A Matter of Latitude by Isobel Blackthorn

To read the first chapter for free, head to:
https://www.nextchapter.pub/books/a-matter-of-latitude-
thriller-set-in-spain

ABOUT THE AUTHOR

Isobel Blackthorn is an award-winning author of unique and engaging fiction. She writes gripping mysteries, dark psychological thrillers, and historical and literary fiction. Isobel was shortlisted for the Ada Cambridge Prose Prize 2019 for her biographical short story 'Nothing to Declare', a version of the first chapter of her forthcoming family history novel. Isobel holds a PhD for her research on the works of Theosophist Alice A. Bailey, the 'Mother of the New Age'. She is the author of *The Unlikely Occultist: a biographical novel of Alice A. Bailey*. With a grand passion for the Canary Islands lodged in her heart, Isobel continues to write novels set on Lanzarote and Fuerteventura.

BOOKS BY THE AUTHOR

The Drago Tree

Nine Months of Summer

A Perfect Square

All Because of You

The Cabin Sessions

The Legacy of Old Gran Parks

Twerk

The Unlikely Occultist

A Matter of Latitude

Clarissa's Warning

A Prison in the Sun

Voltaire's Garden
ISBN: 978-4-86747-904-9

Published by
Next Chapter
1-60-20 Minami-Otsuka
170-0005 Toshima-Ku, Tokyo
+818035793528

29th May 2021